Dominance Th(

James C

www.BehaveTech.com

Dominance and Dogs
ISBN 978-0-9738369-4-3
Published by BehaveTech Publishing (www.BehaveTech.com),
Ottawa Ontario Canada
Copyright © 2008 by James O'Heare. All rights reserved. No part of this book may be reproduced or transmitted in any form or by any means, electronic or mechanical, including photocopying, recording, or by an information storage or retrieval system, without permission in writing from the author.

Other Books by James O'Heare

Aggressive Behavior in Dogs
The Dog Aggression Workbook
Separation Distress and Dogs
Raw Meat Diets for Cats and Dogs?

Dedication

I dedicate this book to all the dogs who have been mistreated as a result of the idea of social dominance.

TABLE OF CONTENTS

Table of Contents 1
   PREFACE 2
   INTRODUCTION 3
   INTRODUCTION TO THE SECOND EDITION 3
Part 1. Sociability and Conflict 4
   EVOLUTION 4
   SOLITARY VS. GROUP SURVIVAL STRATEGIES 7
      Eusociality 7
      Aggregations 8
      Societies 8
   SOCIETAL LIVING 8
   PHYSIOLOGICAL MODULATION OF CONFLICT 11
   GENERAL CLARIFICATIONS 12
      Dominance Status, Dominance Rank and Dominance Hierarchy 12
      Social Dominance as Relationship vs. Trait 12
Part 2. What is Social Dominance? 14
   WHAT IS SOCIAL DOMINANCE AND OF WHAT VALUE IS IT? 14
      Methods 15
      Results 23
      Analysis 33
      Discussion 45
      Conclusion 49
Part 3. Dominance and Companion Dogs 50
   CRITICISMS OF SOCIAL DOMINANCE 50
      Contextual Complexity Reduces Predictive Value. 50
      Artificial Social Dominance Hierarchies Generated by Captivity- and
      Crowding-Induced Stress 51
      Overemphasis on Aggression 52
      Who Determined Contest Behavior? 53
      Wide Variety of Strategies and Social Structures 53
      Comparing Wolves and Dogs 54
   WITHIN AND BETWEEN SPECIES SOCIAL DOMINANCE 56
      Dog – Dog Social Dominance Relationships 56
      Companion Dog – Dog Relationships 58
      Dog – Human Dominance Relationships 59
      Social Dominance Fosters Adversarial Relationships Between Dogs and
      Their Guardians 60
      Dominance and Aggression 61
   ALTERNATIVE APPROACHES TO EXPLAINING, PREDICTING AND CHANGING THE
   SOCIAL BEHAVIOR OF DOGS 63
   CONCLUSION 66
Bibliography 68

Preface

My goal in writing this small book will be to explore the notion of social dominance in significant depth and then to explore it in relation to domestic dogs. I will attempt to describe the notion and research that has been done in this area and evaluate it. This is meant to contribute to the present ongoing debate surrounding this topic and criticism is welcome.

Part one of this book will be on sociability and the nature of conflicts of interests among members of social groups. Part two will present the results of my research into what social dominance is and of what value it is. Part three will address some general criticisms of social dominance, and will apply what we have reviewed to dogs. In this section I will present an argument for abandoning theories of social dominance in companion dogs in favor of a behavioral approach to explaining, predicting and changing behavior. It is important that we set the stage for our discussion of social dominance in dogs by looking closely at the science and research behind it first. You will not see the word "dog" too many times in part one and two, but rest assured we will address dogs in part three, once we have come to a better understanding of what social dominance is and why we have such an idea.

Many references will be made to research. Generally, when I do not specify the species in question it is because the comments or research are referring generally to society forming species generally and not to a specific species.

Some of the discussion makes reference to ethological or behavioral terminology that might not be easily accessible to the general public without a little background in social dominance or the principles of learning but most of the content should be readable to a layperson reader. Eaton (2002) provides a concise discussion of social dominance that I would recommend for the layperson that wants a short easy to read document. The present work will be an attempt to explore these topics in a more academic context and hence might be a tougher read for some.

Introduction

What is social dominance? What is it specifically not, and what place does it have in understanding or changing the social behavior of companion dogs? These are the questions that will be addressed in this book. Social dominance is one of the most controversial subjects in the dog behavior field right now and deserving of a thorough exploration of the notion itself and the ramifications it realizes. My thesis will be that while the notion of social dominance holds potential for value in a social psychology and ethology context, it is an insidious idea with regards to explaining and changing behavior between companion dogs or dogs and people — that it should be abandoned completely in that context in favor of a more efficient, effective and scientifically defensible behavioral approach.

Introduction to the Second Edition

In the second edition, I have completely replaced part 2 with the findings of my dissertation research project on social dominance. In part three, I have shifted from a report approach to an expositional argument for abandoning social dominance in favor of a behavioral approach. The work is significantly longer and much more in-depth.

PART 1. SOCIABILITY AND CONFLICT

The development of sociability in individuals and populations is influenced by both learning and evolutionary factors. In this section I will review the basic principles of the theory of evolution so that we can understand better the role that evolution plays in contributing to sociability and group social living. This section will also explore how social structure may have developed through time. The learning components of sociability will be discussed after that and throughout the book.

Evolution

Evolution refers to changes in allele frequencies within a population of organisms over time. It is important to understand that individuals do not evolve (an individual's alleles generally remain stable through their lifetime)—but rather populations evolve (the allele frequencies within the population change as members are born or die).

In order to understand this topic, we need to define some terms—genotype, phenotype, allele, gene, and natural selection. A distinction must be made between an individual's genotype and phenotype. A genotype for a trait consists of the specific alleles that an individual possesses related to that trait. We use the term phenotype to describe how that trait is expressed or displayed. The genotype is the genetic blueprint and provides the instructions for the organism to produce proteins, which then produce structures of the body. A genotype is the underlying genetic basis for a phenotype. The proteins interact with each other and with the environment to form larger, more complex structures. These proteins and structures are referred to as phenotypes. They are the physical, observable traits produced by the genotype. The genotype (the blueprint) provides the potential for a range of possible phenotypes (the result you see). What is actually "expressed" within that range of potentiality will depend on how the environment interacts with the structures as they develop. For example the genotype for a person may optimally specify growth to a 6'4" tall adult. But if, as a child the individual is malnourished he may only grow to 5'6". This, from an evolutionary perspective, is an environmental interaction, affecting the expression of the genotype for that individual. Environmental influences operating at key developmental stages can significantly modify or limit the expression of the genotype. Whether the phenotype dictated by the genotype is "expressed" depends on the effects of the environmental influences.

Likewise, in a social context, a dog might possess the genotype for a high-level social attraction trait but if the puppy is prevented from imprinting and socializing or has traumatizing social experiences the phenotype may not reflect the genetic potential. Instead the expressed phenotype may reflect the other extreme in the range of potential behaviors and the dog could be decidedly antisocial. If that individual was genetically predisposed to being resiliently social they will likely be more social than if the exact same developmental deficits and traumas were inflicted upon a dog that is not so predisposed. The genotype sets the range of potential outcomes and the environment determines the result.

Because it is often misunderstood, we need to explain the difference between a gene and an allele. A gene is merely a location on a chromosome, while alleles are the coded information in the gene. It is possible for there to be one allele but more often than not, there are a variety of alleles for any particular gene. We often hear of "gene pools" and "gene frequencies" but in fact the gene is merely the location where the alleles are found so it is more accurate to refer to allele pools and allele frequencies. The gene (location) is generally the same from generation to generation but the alleles (coded variation found for that gene) can change from generation to generation and this change is what evolution is about.

There are several reasons why allele frequencies may change from generation to generation including mutation, natural selection, genetic drift, recombination and gene flow. Of primary interest to us here is natural selection. Natural selection refers to the environmental influence on the reproductive success of some individual members of a population. If this environmental selective pressure acts differentially on members of the population, some will have greater reproductive success than others. Hence the subsequent generation will have more offspring derived from the more reproductively successful individuals of previous generations. The alleles from the reproductively successful organisms will be increased in the next generation and the alleles of the reproductively unsuccessful will alternatively decrease. Within a population, variation in traits is common. Examples of traits that might be important to sociability include variable aggressiveness, size, confidence, and prey preference. Natural selection operates on this variation in traits (phenotypes) within individuals within a population. To the extent that the traits are heritable determines whether that population evolves. Adaptive variations of traits are passed on at a greater rate than maladaptive traits (traits selected against), and with this inheritance come changes in the frequencies of the alleles involved from one generation to the next in the population. This is evolution.

The observed characteristics that contribute to an organism's reproductive fitness are called phylogenetic adaptations (or commonly just adaptations) to the extent that they are heritable. Those traits, which contribute to reproductive fitness are said to be adaptive.

Another term intricately related to adaptation and natural selection is fitness. Fitness is often thought to refer to physical fitness but from an evolutionary perspective, fitness refers to reproductive fitness—the reproductive success of a particular individual relative to the average reproductive success of the population as a whole (Siiter, 1999). Without reference to reproduction, the notion of fitness is meaningless within the theory of evolution. It is through variation in reproductive fitness that allele frequencies change within the allele pool and the population evolves. Those individuals who possess the variations most adaptive to the environment will tend to produce more progeny as nature applies a selective pressure against those with maladaptive traits. Those animals that possess maladaptive traits will tend to produce fewer progeny; many simply die off without producing any progeny. Natural selection acts to remove deleterious alleles from the allele pool and hence adaptive alleles become relatively predominant—they are simply what are left.

A Primer on the Theory of Evolution by Natural Selection

Because Evolution and Natural Selection are so commonly misunderstood, I would like to provide a quick and concise summary as a stand alone box for easy reference and as a different manner of explaining it, hopefully, to help with understanding it.

Evolution by natural selection is simply about differential reproductive success and the changes in allele frequencies as a result of this. Some individuals reproduce more than others. Their traits are said to be adaptive. Genes (genotype) contribute to the mechanisms that establish physical and behavioral traits (phenotype). When one individual is more reproductively successful than another individual is, the traits that the successful individual possesses become more prominent in the population while those of the less reproductively successful individual become less prominent (to the extent that they have heritable components). In this way, traits become more and less probable in the future within the population of individuals. Remember, populations evolve, not individuals. When we say that nature selects for certain traits we do not mean to imply any intention, or direction. Actually, when we say that the nature selects for certain traits (behavioral or physical) we mean that in a given environment, certain traits will be more adaptive than others. Those traits that are not adaptive lead to the animal reproducing less, and in that sense, we say the adaptive traits were selected for.

There is no grand purpose to evolution, nor directionality and it is not about "survival" per se. It is about reproduction. Fitness does not refer to one's physical fitness. It refers to various measures of reproductive success (e.g., number of offspring, or number of grandchildren). Evolution does not imply that a given trait is the best possible solution even for the environment it evolved in. It just implies that in that particular environment, some trait that was present was more successful than other traits present. So many people want to read more into it than that and most textbooks do not help. It is actually very simple. The consequences might be far reaching but the mechanism of the theory is simple.

Here are the basic principles of evolution through natural selection:

- Traits (phenotypes) are variable
- Some traits (phenotypes) have heritable components
- Some individuals are reproductively more successful than others
- As a result, allele frequencies change in populations through time as new individuals are born and others die

---

In the context of the evolution of social behavior, such environmental features as food preference and predators are often important elements of the selective pressure for sociability. If the predator preys on large animals, traits that encourage group cooperative effort might be adaptive. For example if wolves hunt for bison, traits that encourage group cooperation might be expected to be adaptive. This is because alone they are likely to be unsuccessful and their reproductive fitness goes down. Dogs, on the other hand, do not hunt large animals. All else being equal, we would expect group cooperation to be less adaptive in this case. It is in this way that the environment applies selective pressure for certain traits and the successful variations increase the allele frequency for those traits and the population evolves their unique sociability. Likewise, if a skilled hunter might prey upon them, traits that encourage group living might be adaptive. For example in some populations of wild dogs, wolves are the important predator. It might be adaptive for dogs that face this pressure to form a group. More animals in the group means a better chance of spotting the predator in time to initiate a defense and the defense is likely to be more successful. Many of these traits have some heritable component and to the extent that they do these environmental features may create a selective pressure for sociability and society formation.

Solitary vs. Group Survival Strategies

Some animals, such as many insects, form a eusocial structure. Some other animals congregate in loose herds. In other species, societies are formed. In some societies, families constitute the entire group while in others, multiple families or extended families form the groups. Yet others are combinations of families and unrelated individuals. The makeup of a society is determined by the natural history and particular circumstances of that population. Traits have evolved to promote this way of life because those who have participated in the society lived to pass on their genes while the loners died off (or at least failed to reproduce). Learning and cultural transmission likely contributes to this process.

In certain circumstances, a species evolves to live a solitary life. In these situations the organism is able to survive without facing the necessity to compete with a group for these resources. In these situations solitary living is adaptive. In others, it would not be. These animals usually meet seasonally for breeding purposes and then go their separate ways again. Certain large cats and bears live in this manner.

In other instances, there is selective pressure for group living because of the circumstances of the environment. In these cases, the solitary animals are less successful at reproducing and the group living members of the population are more successful. Those traits that contributed to group living strategies become more frequent in the allele pool. In this way group living is selected for. There are certain broad categories of group living strategies. They are eusociality, aggregation and society.

Eusociality

Eusociality is common in insects. In this system of group living only a small number (e.g., the queen) reproduces. In these caste structures there are categories of members. Some typical castes are reproducers, workers, hive defenders, and brooders.

Aggregations

Aggregations are loose groups of animals that stay together but do not form definite structure, organization or communication (Siiter, 1999). Examples would be herds of cows or some schools of fish. Generally, they group for defensive reasons. Group living offers increased vigilance, defense, and food gathering (Siiter, 1999).

Societies

Societies are more organized groups, which are often characterized by some division of labor, communication, and stability of composition of group resistance of intrusion into the group by others (Siiter, 1999). These groups are more cooperative in nature.

Societal Living

Evolution is a mechanism that allows changes to take place from one generation to the next and for the species to adapt to its environment (phylogenetic adaptation). Learning and choice behavior allows for the individual, in his or her own lifetime, to adapt to a variable and dynamic environment (ontogenetic adaptation). Of course learning, itself, is a genetically evolved biological mechanism (Skinner, 1984 as cited in Chance, 1988) and is constrained by the individual's genetic makeup.

Within societies, the benefits of group living usually outweigh the benefits of solitary life for the individual. It is generally more advantageous for the animal to remain in the group than to become solitary. There are many mechanisms that hold groups together, which are selected for as the population evolves. Communication systems allow members of the group to send and understand signals and hence manipulate each other's behavior to best suit their individual needs. It is important to remember that it is the individual and their traits that are selected for and not those of the group as a unit. Each member is appropriately self-interested and acts to increase the frequency of his own alleles by surviving and reproducing. This is not to suggest a conscious effort on the part of the animal. Another trait, memory, allows each member to learn from social encounters and to recognize other members individually. By being able to learn and remember other members, they can better behave in a way that maximizes their own alleles.

Now I will provide the basic reasoning for social dominance within this evolutionary and social context. Within a society, group members compete with one another for access to resources including food and mates. Agonistic behavior is a major means of settling these competitions. But active aggression is risky and hence other strategies are selected for. If two wolves ripped each other to shreds every time there was a single piece of food to eat, the pack would be gone in a very short period of time and the benefits of group living would be gone. The mechanisms of communication, memory, learning ability etc. allow for competition without this high risk. When two members face each other (usually at the beginning of their relationship), they assess each other for their likelihood of winning a direct confrontation with their opponent—they size each other up. In most cases, they are evaluating the opponent's ability in relation to their own. They are looking at size, condition, weaponry and motivational cues. Each member may try to look as big and healthy as possible and as motivated as they can. They will display their weaponry. Their fight is ritualized so as to prevent damage that would result from an actual fight. Those that fight when it is unnecessary, risk damage or death. Fewer of these individual's alleles are passed on and so it is not adaptive. In some cases, one member will admit defeat prior to a fight. They may simply retreat or they may present species specific "submissive" or "appeasement" signals. These signals indicate to the opponent that they do not wish to fight and they will cease competition for the resource in question. This usually is the case when assessment does not clearly suggest who the winner would be. In this case, a winner usually emerges who gets the resource in question. So far, there is nothing controversial in the description of this process (although different theoretical orientations would describe it in different terms; this was an ethological account). In some formulations of social dominance, we might proclaim the winner dominant, but in others we need data from more than one contest. The problem comes when we want a theory to help us explain, predict or change the future relationships within the group that revolve around these competitions. This is what the notion of social dominance is for.

After two members of a society have competed, they may learn from that confrontation. They recognize the individual and remember whether they won or lost in the confrontation. They learn more from that confrontation than they did in their initial assessment and that new and more complete information helps them decide how to act in future encounters with that individual. The winner of a contest experiences a surge of testosterone and the loser experiences a surge in corticosterone—the winner is encouraged and the loser is discouraged physiologically. What we find in some species (*Rivulus marmoratus*) is that winners tend to continue winning and losers tend to continue to lose (Chase, Bartolomeo, & Dugatkin, 1994; Hsu & Wolf, 2001). Losers of recent contests tend to decrease their initiation of future contests although this was not the case for winners (Hsu & Wolf, 2001). Losers also tend to actually lose these future contests (Chase et al., 1994). The winners were not appreciably more likely to initiate future contests, but, if they do initiate a contest, they are significantly more likely to initiate with an actual attack (Hsu & Wolf, 2001). This was not the case for losers. If a ritualized display is used to challenge a winner they are significantly more likely to respond with an actual attack (Hsu & Wolf, 2001). The importance of these experiences becomes less significant once a fight has been escalated, likely because the information drawn from the actual fight is more valuable and useful than the previous experience (Hsu & Wolf, 2001). It may be that these winner and loser effects actually play a significant role in predicting future contests. "Among closely matched pairs, dominance of one individual over another might be determined by which has just successfully attacked some other individual, rather than by any qualities that could have been measured before the individuals were assembled to form a hierarchy." (Chase et al., 1994) These future encounters seem to be largely guided by the behavior of the loser. The loser often displays submissive signals immediately upon encountering the winner. The winner usually accepts this and wins the present competition by default without escalation. You might be wondering how this could be selected for. First, there is more than one strategy for getting these resources. They can be "sneaky" rather than get into a face-to-face competition for it, or they might employ some other strategy. For example, in certain frog species, weaker males may position themselves just outside of the dominant male's territory and as the females are attracted to the dominant male's mating calls the "satellite male" intercepts the incoming females (Stebbins & Cohen, 1995, pp. 161-162). In this way, he avoids losses due to being subordinate and still manages to reproduce. The losers often do manage to reproduce and hence their strategy becomes stable also. But perhaps more direct is that it is simply better to defer and live to try to reproduce another day, than to fight a likely losing battle and risk serious harm or death. The latter option is not likely adaptive.

Losers (and it's important to note that the term is used in a technical, and not derogatory manner by researchers) have two options open to them: they can accept their loser status and wait for their day in the sun while still making use of alternative strategies to gain resources, or they can become a solitary animal and go off on their own. In some cases, becoming solitary can mean that this individual will have better access to resources and mating opportunities. In these particular environmental conditions, dispersal is likely to take place. For example, you could have a wolf that occupies the lowest rank position in the group hierarchy, gets very little food, no mating opportunities etc. In that case, if predators are not a large problem and food is somewhat readily available and easy to get without group-coordinated efforts, the wolf may decide to go it alone. This may or may not work out for him or her. You might even have a situation in which the alpha wolf harasses another wolf out of the group and he or she is forced to become solitary. In most cases, members of societies do not choose to become solitary. In most cases, there are good reasons why the animal is a member of a group and even occupying a low rank can often present better odds for food and mating opportunities than going it alone. The group offers a lot. Also, in most species, the losers do get the opportunity to at least eat, even if the winner controls it. Relationships will usually form in this manner between each dyad (group of two animals) within the group. Notions of social dominance will often try to explain, describe or predict these relationships.

It is important to note that each species is different, as was stressed above, and the social structure and mechanisms of each species will be unique to its evolutionary past and the present circumstances of the group. Other complicating factors can include groups that do not follow simple winner-loser systems. In many animals (including many primates), coalitions can be formed in which those animals who are always losers become winners when they are in the presence of certain other animals that will help them. A team of losers can defeat a winner and bring complexity to the relationship dynamics of the group. You may also find that in certain situations, a particular animal is always a winner but then in another context he is always a loser. You may also find that as incentives change, so too do wining and losing frequencies. If in a particular contest in which a clear winner / loser relationship exists and the loser is particularly motivated that time for some reason (perhaps he is very hungry while the winner is full) then the usual loser may win that context. So how are we going to keep track of all this complexity and how valid and reliable can these theories be in the face of such complex and difficult to test circumstances? We will explore that question in detail in part two and three.

Physiological Modulation of Conflict

Physiology plays a role in modulating social dominance relationships. Stress related corticosterone and aggression-modulating testosterone are highly influential in this regard. It is not a simple relationship though. Testosterone, for example, not only affects behavior but also responds to it (Mazure, 1998). Mazure makes two key observations on how testosterone interacts with behavior: "First, testosterone rises in the face of a challenge, as if it were an anticipatory response to impending competition. Second, after the competition, testosterone rises in winners and declines in losers." (Mazure, 1998) It is accepted that testosterone increases aggressiveness (Rowell, 1974).

Mazure (1998) offers this primer in testosterone:

Testosterone is the primary androgen, a class of steroid hormone that develops and maintains masculine features. Although testosterone is made in the adrenal cortex and ovary of females, it is produced in far greater amounts by the Leydig cells of the testis. Testosterone in men is secreted into the bloodstream in spurts, so measured levels can change considerably within a few minutes.

In human males, circulating testosterone is correlated with dominance, aggression and social norm breaking (Mazure, 1998).

It has been found that in athletes, testosterone rises prior to competition and it remains high in the winner for an hour or two after competition (Mazure, 1998). Similar results have been found in nonphysical, more symbolic status oriented competitive events such as in chess competition (Mazure). Losing seems to have a hormone-depressive effect (Mazure). In the context of physiology, one might say that in dominance contests, one competitor is acting to out-stress the opponent (Mazure) in a war of attrition of sorts. The physiological response to stress (which can, in this context, be thought of as the polar opposite to a winning testosterone effect) can be divided into two processes—the emergency response (increases sympathetic nervous activity and secretion of adrenalin and noradrenalin) and a longer-term response (increased adrenocorticotrophin secretion and consequent release of glucocorticoids), called the a general adaptation syndrome (GAS) (Deag, 1977).

To summarize, testosterone present in winners tends to make winners competitive, reactive and aggressive while glucocorticoids influence losers, suppressing or inhibiting them (Hsu & Wolf, 2001).

It can be seen from this research that there are physiological components to the winning and losing effects that are also complimented by the process of assessment and learning. All processes seem to compliment each other in modulating behavior such that those who are best suited to being a winner continue to be winners and those less suited tend to remain losers. Of course this is all in the context of motivating variables, which change through time and in different contexts.

General Clarifications

Before we move on to part two, in which we will explore the various notions of social dominance, I would like to clear up some common misunderstandings regarding terminology and then discuss the debate regarding whether social dominance is a trait or a description of a relationship as this is another common source of confusion.

Dominance Status, Dominance Rank and Dominance Hierarchy

In popular dog behavior literature, terms such as status, rank and hierarchy are used either interchangeably or uncritically. For clarity sake, it is important to distinguish these terms. Dominance status refers to the position of an individual animal in a dyad, and can either be dominant or subordinate according to the direction of the statistical significant outcomes of contest interactions (Drews, 1993). Dominance rank refers to the position of an individual in a dominance hierarchy (Drews, 1993). Status can be determined by measuring dyadic agonistic outcomes. Rank can be determined by measuring the outcomes of all possible dyads within a group. A resulting hierarchy can be linear or nonlinear. A linear hierarchy is one in which there is a despot leader who dominates all other members, and a next lowest ranking member dominates all other members except the higher ranking animal etc. In other words A dominates all animals, B dominates all animals except A, C dominates all animals except A and B etc. A nonlinear hierarchy would be that which is less stable and has exceptions to the above transitive rule.

Social Dominance as Relationship vs. Trait

The debate on whether social dominance is a heritable trait or a measure of the relationship between two individuals has been intense (e.g. Moore, 1990; Moore, 1991; Capitanio, 1991; Barrette, 1993; Drews, 1993). It is generally agreed now that dominance refers to a relationship between two animals.

After stripping away the misunderstandings, it would seem that it is now generally agreed that social dominance is not an individual trait but rather a relationship at the dyadic level and hence not directly heritable. "One reason why dominance cannot be inherited is that dominance is a property of a relationship not a trait of an individual." (Barrette, 1993) But this does not mean that genetic inheritance cannot exert an influence upon the dyadic relationship. Scott and Fuller (1965) have carried out perhaps the largest scale study of the genetics of social behavior in companion dogs and it is clear from that and other research that genetics has some influence on traits that contribute to dominance relationships (Scott & Fuller, p. 165). Of course if one were to accept one of the definitions that identifies dominance as an individual trait then we would be able to select for dominance, by definition. If we accept a definition of dominance that is relationship-based then while we agree that relative social relationships cannot be selected for, we can also agree that certain individual traits can influence or contribute to social relationships. Drews (1993) offers this: "On the other hand, breeding experiments suggest that there is a genetic component to *determinants* of rank, when dominance is defined as an attribute of relationships." [emphasis added] (Dewsbury, 1990). To the extent that these individual traits are heritable we can attribute certain influences to genetic inheritance.

Some features that may have heritable components and which then influence individual behavior and hence social relationships may be size, and aggressiveness to mention two. In many cases, an animal will regard relative size in their assessment. That assessment could lead to submissive deference without escalation and hence influence the resulting relationship. If a context results due to a close match in weaponry, size, age and other variables, the animal who is most inclined to escalate quickly and fiercely is likely to be victorious and future outcomes may be affected, both in terms of this animal being more likely to win but also in terms of others deferring without escalation via learning and individual recognition.

PART 2. WHAT IS SOCIAL DOMINANCE?

As mentioned, social dominance was developed to help describe, explain and/or predict the relationships between members of organized societies of animals; most recently, to explain why we see relatively little damage due to aggression among social predators. Pierre Huber first recognized dominance orders in 1802 in bumblebees (Wilson, 1975). Later (1922) it was proposed for vertebrates by Schjelderupp-Ebbe and has undergone many revisions and reformulations since then (Wilson, 1975). Schjelderupp-Ebbe's work was in describing the social behavior of chickens, which form simple linear hierarchies of social status. Many investigators have since made claims that social dominance is a universal feature of social relationships (Allee & Emerson, 1949 as cited in Wilson, 1975). Since 1922, investigators have studied this idea in application to many other species. As they face complications they have had to adjust or reformulate the theory or otherwise add to it in an ad hoc manner in order to make it fit their observations. On top of that, different researchers and theorists have attacked the problem from different theoretical approaches and with different criteria of value. The result of all these years of research, controversy and debate has been widespread confusion and misunderstanding. Often researchers argue over social dominance without a clear operational definition and perhaps with different definitions in mind. Contradictory experimental results probably reflect differing premises and assumptions, and add to the muddy waters that are social dominance.

Does social dominance exist? The idea exists. The real question is does it reflect a real phenomenon in reality and provide useful explanatory power? Can we use it as a theory to generate hypotheses and come to understand social relationships better? That is the real question. It is in that context that we examine the idea of social dominance. There is still no agreement regarding the meaning of "dominance" (Drews, 1993). In part two, we will examine various categories and definitions of social dominance as well as their value in great detail.

The section below is based on a research dissertation project I undertook and was published as an article in the Journal of Applied Companion Animal Behavior (O'Heare, 2007).

What is Social Dominance and of What Value is it?

The field of social dominance is thus far a quagmire. Despite a vast literature on the topic, no agreement has been reached on exactly what is meant by social dominance. Those notions that exist often lack coherence or clearly stated assumptions and prediction.

The purpose of this analysis is to address the questions of what social dominance is, as a notion, and of what value it is.

The term dominant is used generally to refer to the individual who exerts the most influence or control over others; who rules or governs; who surpasses others in power; who is commanding and prominent; who is the more important, strong or noticeable. The most common notion found in definitions of dominant was exercising the most influence or control.

Animals can achieve dominance in different ways. The individual who maintains the most influence and control of either others or circumstances may do so by brute force or by cultivating alliances and coalitions. Since different measures of dominance do not intercorrelate well, perhaps dominance refers to the individual who is most competent at exerting control. There may be different manners of achieving that control for different species.

Social dominance should be distinguished from the various other concepts of dominance (e.g., competitive dominance). Social dominance should apply to social relationships and deal with interpersonal exertion of influence and control. Social relationships are recognized "when two (or more) individuals interact regularly or periodically over an extended period of time, recognize each other, and remember the results of past encounters" (Hand, 1986).

Limited resources can create a conflict of interest between animals within social relationships, which sets the occasion for competition. Aggression is useful in competition, but it must be weighed in a cost–benefit analysis with the value of the relationship and the risk associated with use of aggression. In a competitive situation, we would expect some kind of regulation of escalated overt aggression; this might be the use of assessment and display in conventionalized interactions, whereby each opponent gathers information on which competitor would win if aggression were escalated. The competitors may use immediate information (e.g., display) for this, but they might also make use of the history of previous encounters with the other individual to assess their likelihood of winning this resource. They would likely balance this assessment and the attendant risk with the value of the resource in question and decide whether to defer or escalate if necessary. In this environment, we would expect conventions or rules to emerge in which at least some escalated competitions would be settled via preemptive deference rather than overt aggression. This seems to be the basis for social dominance based on my review of the literature. But a formal, coherent theory is more than a plausible story. My goal is to explore the various and disparate notions of social dominance so that theory building can move forward.

Methods

I performed a thorough review of the literature, identifying 18 commonly discussed notions of social dominance. The notions were selected based on the criteria that they: (a) are commonly discussed notions in the literature; (b) are social, in the sense that they require some form of interactions between individuals (as distinguished from some forms of competitive dominance); and (c) deal with dominance in the sense that they involve the influence and control exerted by individuals over other individuals.

I will use the term notion to describe most of the treatments of dominance, since I have not yet determined whether they are ideas, definitions, explanations, hypotheses, models or some other type of utterance.

Analysis Protocol

Different types of notions have different purposes and address different questions, and should be evaluated with specific criteria according to the purpose of the notion. Given this, the various notions were classified by type prior to evaluation and then evaluated in accordance with criteria appropriate to their classification. Systematic analysis of the various notions allows the research questions to be addressed.

The protocol illustrated in Figure 1 shows the analysis in detail. The 1 level shape indicates the pool of notions considered. The 2-series level represents the first stage in the analysis—determination of whether the notion is a denotative definition, connotative definition or explanation, as well as initial filters for congruence, and whether the notion relates to social relationships or not. The 3-series level represents the analysis stage, in which each surviving notion is evaluated for fatal flaws and finally assessed for value.

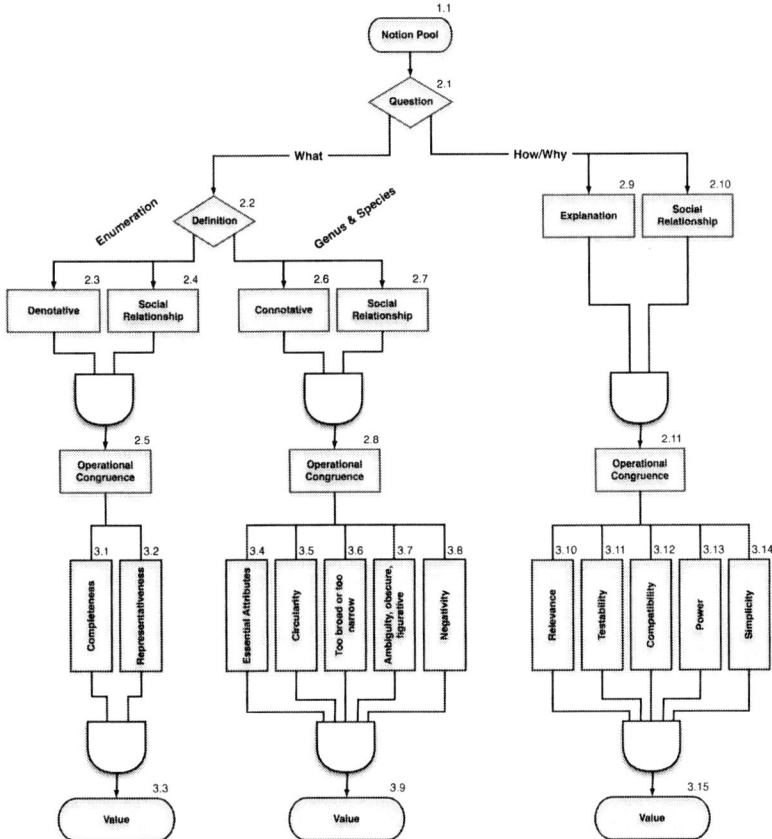

Figure 1. Algorithm outlining each step available for analyzing each notion. The shield-shaped boxes, with more than one line entering and only one exiting, are logical "and-gates." Each of the criteria immediately preceding the and-gate from which a line comes must be met in order for the notion to continue through the and-gate. If one or more criteria are not met, the notion is discarded at the and-gate.

Definition/Explanation Distinction

The most fundamental way to identify the most basic distinctions is to divide the notions into categories based on the questions that the notions are meant to answer. The most basic questions applicable to the topic are what and how/why. This distinction represents the two broad categories "definition" and "explanation," respectively (Fogelin, 1987; Little, Groarke, & Tindale, 1998). The what-question (definition) asks what is social dominance. A definition identifies the essential properties of a term and differentiates it from other terms. The how-question (explanation) usually asks how does social dominance operate. It can also ask more specific how-questions about elements of dominance. The why-question (explanation) usually asks why does social dominance exist or some more specific why-question about an element of social dominance. An explanation is a group of statements from which the thing to be explained can logically be inferred and whose acceptance removes or diminishes its problematic or puzzling character. Therefore, notions were first classified as either definition or explanation by determining the question they provide an answer for.

If the authors proposed a definition that stands alone or is otherwise distinct from their explanation, these were considered separately as a definition and as an explanation. If, on the other hand, the definition is implicit in the explanation or otherwise indistinguishable from the explanation, it was treated as a facet of the explanation and classified as an explanation only.

Definitions (the What Notions) (Box 2.2)

Definitions are intended to clarify the meaning of a word, term, concept or idea. In defining a term, we can focus on the denotation or connotation of the word. I based my classification on these two techniques, classifying each definition as either denotative or connotative, then evaluating it and finally discussing it in order to find its utility as a definition.

Denotative definitions tell us what a thing is by enumerating objects that constitute the class in question; they can be a complete enumeration or a partial enumeration (Copi, 1986, p. 149).

Connotative definitions tell us what a thing is by identifying attributes shared by, and only by, objects contained in the class in question. Connotative definitions are achieved by naming the "class" of which the term is a subclass, and then identifying the difference (characteristics) that distinguishes its members from other members within that class (Copi, 1986, p. 157).

If a definition enumerates a list of objects to define itself, it was classified a denotative definition. If the definition identifies the class and characteristics of the term in question, it was classified a connotative definition. If a combination definition was identified, the denotative definition was retained as a denotative definition and the connotative definition was retained as a connotative definition.

Relevance to Social Relationships (Box 2.4 for Denotative and 2.7 for Connotative)

Next, I assessed each notion for its relevance to "social relationships." I discarded those that are irrelevant and retained for evaluation those that are relevant.

Social, in the context of the term social dominance, refers to the quality of a series of at least two encounters between at least two individuals, such that the information remembered from previous social encounters with that particular individual affects future encounters. The necessary conditions are (a) at least two encounters between at least two individuals and (b) previous encounters affect the outcome of future encounters between two specific individuals. I discarded notions not specifically requiring both of these necessary conditions.

Operational Congruence (Box 2.5 for Denotative and 2.8 for Connotative)

Although worded differently in some cases, some notions of social dominance seem operationally identical. For simplicity's sake, I treated as one those notions surviving the social relationship criterion that were found to be operationally identical to any other notions surviving the social relationship criterion. What is left is a list of distinct definitions of social dominance. This is important for the sake of simplicity and clarity. I treated as one those definitions that identify the same attributes, either with identical words or synonyms or by way of inference. I then treated as one, with name preference going to the notion published first, those that are operationally identical.

Evaluation of Denotative Definitions

I then classified the denotative definitions by degree of completeness in their enumeration, and then by their level of representativeness. I retained those that are reasonably complete and representative with consideration of conventional use of the notion of social dominance. I discarded those that are not. I retained notions meeting all criteria in the denotative definition evaluation (i.e., completeness and representativeness), and discarded those notions that fail one or more of the criteria.

Completeness (Box 3.1)

The more objects that I could identify that should be enumerated within the definition through consideration of conventional notions of the term, the less complete the definition was considered. I discarded those notions that fail this criterion. If I could not identify significantly important objects in the enumeration, where they should be, in the context of conventional use of the term, social dominance, I discarded the notion because it fails the completeness criterion.

Representativeness (Box 3.2)

With consideration of the conventional use of the term, I evaluated each definition for representativeness by efforts to find unrepresented objects. If significant misrepresentations could be identified, the notion failed the represenativeness criterion. The more unrepresented objects, the less representative the definition. I discarded those notions that fail this criterion.

Value of Denotative Definitions (Box 3.3)

I assessed the general value, or usefulness, of the denotative definitions of social dominance that have been retained. In a broad sense, the surviving definitions are free of serious flaws. This final stage should refine the value assessment by taking the most useful denotative definitions of social dominance available and clarifying their value more particularly and precisely. Below, I discuss the surviving definitions in terms of how complete and representative they are, and how consistent the definition is with conventional ideas of what social dominance should and should not include.

Evaluation of Connotative Definitions

According to Copi (1986), there are five broad criteria by which to judge the value of connotative definitions (essential attributes, circularity, too broad or too narrow, ambiguous obscure or vague language, negative). The remaining explanations were evaluated based on these five criteria. I retained those notions meeting all criteria in the connotative definition evaluation and discarded those notions that fail one or more of the criteria.

Does the definition state the essential attributes of the subclass? (Box 3.4)

The definition should identify the essence of the meaning of the term. A class only contains the characteristics it contains and none is more essential than another; as used here, identifying the essential characteristics means identifying the conventional connotation by which we decide if an object or situation is defined by the term (Copi, 1986, p. 159). A notion meets the essential-attributes criterion if it is consistent with conventional use of the term social dominance. If I could identify an inconsistency, the notion fails the essential-attributes criteria. I discarded those notions that fail this criterion.

Does the definition avoid circularity? (box 3.5)

"A circular definition is one that assumes a prior understanding of the term being defined" (wikipedia.org1, n.d.). A definition is circular if it uses a synonym or near synonym to define the term (wikipedia.org3, n.d.) or if the description of the term relies on the term itself (Copi, 1986, p. 159). Circularity is similar to tautology. "A tautology is a statement which is true by its own definition, and is therefore fundamentally uninformative. Tautologies use circular reasoning within an argument or statement" (wikipedia.org2, n.d.). If a term is circular, the definition will fail to achieve its purpose of explaining the meaning of the term. If I could identify a circular or tautological definition, the definition failed to pass the "circularity" criteria and was discarded.

Does the definition avoid being neither too broad nor too narrow? (Box 3.6)

A good connotative definition will not include more or fewer things within the class and subclass it lays out than it should to identify the meaning of the term in question. If I could argue in respect to conventional use of the term that a definition contains either too narrow or too broad a definition (in other words, if it includes or excludes things it should not), then it fails to avoid too broad or narrow a definition and I discarded it.

Does the definition avoid ambiguous, obscure or figurative language? (Box 3.7)

If a definition is ambiguous, it fails to fulfill the function of clarifying the meaning of a term. If I could identify ambiguous, obscure or figurative language that significantly hampers the definition, it fails to achieve the appropriate clarity and I discarded it.

Does the definition avoid being negative where it can be affirmative? (Box 3.8)

Some terms, by their nature, require a negative definition. This rule simply requires that, where it is possible to do so, the definition should be a positive rather than negative one. If I could argue that a definition is negative where it should be positive, then it fails to achieve the negativity test and I discarded it.

Value of Connotative Definitions (Box 3.9)

Below, I discuss the retained connotative definitions in terms of identifying what objects they include and exclude. I contrast and compare each surviving connotative definition to the conventional idea of social dominance, and present a qualitative value judgment based on the assessment. I also determine the value of the definition, based on the appropriateness of what is included and excluded from object membership, compared with conventional use of the term social dominance, and with what is useful in a definition.

Explanation (the Why and How Notions)

Unlike definitions, explanations provide understanding by identifying reasons, causes and/or consequences for a thing. An explanation is a group of statements from which the thing to be explained can logically be inferred and whose acceptance removes or diminishes its problematic or puzzling character. An explanation accounts for the conclusion with premises.

Relevance to Social Relationships (Box 2.10)

I handled relevance to social relationships in a similar way to relevance for the definitions (see the relevant section above).

Operational Congruence (Box 2.11)

Two explanations are operationally identical if one can generate the same predictions and reference to the same factors meant to explain the same facts. If more than one explanation surviving the social relationship criterion makes the same predictions, they were considered as one, with name preference going to the first notion published.

Evaluation of Explanations

Copi (1986) provides five criteria by which to evaluate the usefulness of explanations. I chose these criteria because they represent a broad and generally agreed upon set of criteria for evaluating definitions and explanations. I retained notions meeting all criteria in the explanation evaluation (i.e., relevance, testability, compatibility with previously well-established hypotheses, predictive or explanatory power, and simplicity), and I discarded those notions that fail one or more of the criteria.

Relevance (Box 3.10)

The fact in question must be deducible from the hypothesis, if not from the hypothesis alone then from the hypothesis and certain causal laws that may be presumed to be highly probable, or from the hypothesis and certain stated assumptions. If the fact in question is not deducible from the model, then it fails to explain the fact. If I could identify relevant facts or propositions presented by the explanation that cannot be inferred from the premises or assumptions of the explanation, I discarded it for violation of the relevance criterion.

Testability (Box 3.11)

For a hypothesis to be valuable scientifically, there must be a way to demonstrate that the hypothesis is not true. If a hypothesis is not refutable, it does not meet this basic requirement of science. If I could identify a plausible method of testing the explanation, the explanation meets the criteria of testability. I discarded those notions that fail this criterion.

Compatibility with previously well-established hypotheses (Box 3.12)

In many cases, if a new hypothesis is incompatible with previously well-established hypotheses, then the new hypothesis is likely less valuable. If I could not identify a previously well-established hypothesis that conflicts with the explanation in question, the explanation meets the criteria of compatibility. I discarded those notions that fail this criterion.

Predictive or explanatory power (Box 3.13)

The range of observable facts that can be deduced from the hypothesis is referred to as its predictive or explanatory power. I evaluated the range of facts or observations explained or predicted by the explanation. If the explanation predicts or explains important and relevant essential aspects of what is considered conventionally to relate to social dominance, then the explanation meets the criterion of predictive or explanatory power. I discarded those notions that fail this criterion.

Simplicity (Box 3.14)

The simplest theory that accounts for all the relevant facts is preferable because it is easier to understand and work with. If an explanation is relatively simple in terms of its number of assumptions, number of propositions and ease of understanding, it meets the criterion of simplicity. If it seems particularly complex, or relies on numerous or questionable assumptions or observations, then it fails to meet this criterion. I discarded those notions that fail this criterion.

Value of Explanations of Social Dominance (Box 3.15)

As with the definitions, I assessed the general worth of the explanations of social dominance that had not been discarded through the analysis. I evaluated surviving explanations to identify what phenomena they might help us explain. Below, I explore benefits and limitations, and I make a qualitative value judgment based on this.

Results

My first task was to identify notions of social dominance that met the criteria outlined above. Below, I very briefly outline some key features of the selected notions of social dominance.

Review of the Literature

1. Privileged role dominance

Wilson (1975) describes a notion of dominance, termed "privileged role dominance" by Drews (1993). The essence of this notion seems to be that, as age increases and developmental stage changes, dominance decreases. Social dominance is said to relate to food or resource transfer and is not related to agonistic contests.

2. Reproductive dominance

Wilson (1975, p. 285) describes a notion of dominance based on observations of various species of paper wasp (Polistes sp.). Wilson outlines four behavioral tactics that may be used, individually or in combination, to contribute to maintaining dominance:

- Dominant individuals demand and receive the greatest share of food when that resource is limited.
- They lay the greatest number of eggs in new brood cells.
- When rivals manage to lay eggs, they eat them.
- They use overt aggression to compete successfully with rivals.

Drews (1993) describes the notion as defining the most reproductively successful as dominant. But reproductive activity is the measure of fitness, which is to be a consequence of aggressive competitive tactics described.

3. Dominance is aggressiveness

This simple notion of dominance suggests that, as aggressiveness increases, so too does dominance (Drews, 1993). This notion addresses the observation that animals that are more aggressive are often able to encourage others to defer to them and are most likely to win competitive encounters. Drews puts the argument in this way:

- The tendency to use overt aggression within a society is variable.
- Those who are more aggressive than a competitor will be the dominant individual in that contest or relationship.
- Those who are not as aggressive will be the subordinates.

4. Dominance is a trait that conveys rank

Baenninger (1981) posits that dominance can be thought of as an intervening variable, and that any given animal might possess some trait or traits—which we will call dominance—that contribute to their willingness to engage in and ability to win competitive encounters with other individuals. If the individual wins a statistically significant number of contests with a variety of other individuals, then we infer that this individual possesses more of the trait called dominance. Baenninger proposes assertiveness or aggressiveness as possible synonyms for traits that may contribute to "dominance." Baenninger points out that this empirically based prediction of future outcomes does nothing to help us explain the process, as a theoretical prediction would.

5. Winner is dominant—loser is subordinate

This simple notion suggests that dominance is merely a synonym for winning, and subordinate is a synonym for the loser in any given dyadic encounter, regardless of whether the contest is escalated or not (Drews, 1993). Once an outcome for a particular contest is determined, the dominance or subordination is determined for that contest.

6. Successful combatant

This notion of dominance proposes that the individual who wins one or more contests by either display or escalation of aggression is dominant over their opponent (Drews, 1993). The individual most willing to escalate and who is the most aggressive tends to win and hence be dominant. This is similar to Parker's (1974) notion of resource holding power (RHP) in which the individual most able to continue the contest for the longest is the winner and hence the dominant individual. In this notion of dominance, overall fighting ability is related to dominance; as overall fighting ability increases, so too does dominance. Drews points out that this notion does not imply that escalation is avoided or that individuals recognize each other and incorporate an outcome history into their decision making.

7. Dominance is lack of aggressiveness

Vessey (1981) proposes a notion of dominance that focuses on control of resources through display and submission but does not rely on learning from previous encounters or individual recognition. The notion assumes that, in a contest between two animals, each may assess the opponent through mutual display of fighting ability. Each opponent is able to compare their fighting ability and their opponent's, based on the predictable traits correlated with fighting ability rather than remembering previous outcomes. The opponent who is least likely to win chooses to conserve their energy and submits, while the other gains the resource, thereby controlling the interaction. Control and predictability are necessary, whereas learning or individual recognition is not. Dominance status can be assigned after a single contest (Drews, 1993).

8. Consistent winner of agonistic contests

In repeated agonistic contests, where A consistently defeats B, then A is dominant and B is subordinate (Drews, 1993). This notion requires repeated agonistic contests but does not imply escalated aggression or its avoidance, individual recognition, social relationships, memory or learning. It merely recognizes asymmetry in the proportion of defeats or wins in agonistic encounters.

9. Spheres of dominance / Consistent winner in given context

Hand (1986) defines social dominance as "consistent winning at points of social conflict, regardless of the tactics used" (p. 201). He further defines social conflict as "occurring when the behavior of two (or more) individuals indicate that their motivational priorities are incompatible: they seek the same thing or different things, and both cannot be satisfied" (p. 201). He then defines social dominance further in this way: "[Social dominance]... refers specifically to 'familiar' dyads in which one party follows the 'rule' that it will defer." He identifies two types of social dominance: primary and secondary. Primary social dominance is described as superior force, real or apparent. It can be intrinsic to the individual or derived, due to asymmetries in the relationship between the opponents. Secondary social dominance, on the other hand, depends on leverage rather than superior force. Leverage refers to an asymmetry in the cost of winning. Where the cost for one opponent to win is lower than the cost of the other to win, the first individual possesses a leverage advantage and may consistently win encounters due solely to this mechanism.

Hand (1986) explains that we should expect context-specific payoff asymmetries; that fitness gains can be different in different contexts. The "spheres of dominance" notion presumes that dominance can be different in different contexts, within the definition of conflict and dominance offered above. "Spheres of dominance" classifies social dominance as "pure" or "mixed." Pure dominance/subordination relationships are characterized by one member always being dominant, while the other is always subordinate, across all contexts. Conversely, a mixed social dominance relationship is one in which one member is not always dominant in all contexts. "Spheres of dominance" differentiates social dominance from other forms of conflict resolution. Hand identifies, broadly, three theoretical extremes: relationships with no conflict; relationships in which social dominance is used to determine resource allocation; and egalitarian systems as used to determine resource allocation. An egalitarian system is in operation when conventions are used to avoid conflicts that result in there being a loser and winner, or when wins and losses are achieved equally between both members. When periods of winning by both individuals are short lived, the relationship can be characterized as unresolved. Conventional conflict resolution is thought of as a continuum, with social dominance at one end and egalitarianism at the other end. Empirical observation is used in order to determine where a particular relationship falls on this continuum.

10. Priority of access to resources

Priority of access to resources is generally considered central to a proper notion of dominance. Dominance is used to describe the asymmetry in access to resources. In this argument (Hand, 1986, p. 202), the dominant individual is said to be the one who displaces others from a resource, contests successfully for a resource or maintains possession of a contested resource. In this system, it is not required that aggression be avoided (Drews, 1993). Fighting is also not necessary.

11. Peck order

If A pecks B and B never or seldom pecks A, then A is dominant and B is subordinate. This notion describes a despotic regime or linear hierarchy. It does not allow for nonlinear social structures. Directionality of agonistic behavior is the determining factor in assigning rank.

12. Barrette and Vandal's dominance

Drews (1993) paraphrased Barrette and Vandal's (1986) discussion into a definition in this way: "dominance is an attribute of a relationship between two individuals, whenever an asymmetry in the outcome of agonistic interactions is measured." This is a modification of the peck-order notion in that it allows for more than one interaction type (i.e., agonistic behaviors other than pecking). Drews (1993) further summarizes the modified peck order neatly as characterized by the following:

- Asymmetry in outcome of agonistic encounters.
- Avoidance of escalation mediated by deference.
- Influence of past encounters in subsequent response.

13. Intervening variable

The intervening variable notion of social dominance states specifically that dominance does not exist in the sense that it is directly observable and measurable (i.e., a trait) but rather that it is a construct. Hinde and Datta (1981) propose that social dominance can be a useful explanatory concept. They criticize many commentators on social dominance (e.g., Bernstein, 1981) for confusing empirical notions (what they call data language notions) of social dominance with theoretical notions that explain the phenomenon (what they call theory language notions). They argue that social dominance is not a dependent variable or independent variable. Social dominance is, by this notion, an intervening variable; we observe directionality and we may explain it by postulating the construct of social dominance, similar to how we use the term intelligence to explain certain skills. Hinde and Datta suggest that some independent variables could affect specific interactions and that some may be context dependent. They further propose that these independent variables may interact, which is posited as explaining why merely identifying correlations with these measures and outcomes may not prove useful. They propose certain independent variables (e.g., size, maternal rank, hormonal condition, dyadic experience, age and experience of terrain) as modulating certain intervening variables (e.g., dominance, authority) that then produce the observable dependent variables (e.g., A supplants B, B grooms A, B is submissive to A, A has priority of access, A leads and B follows). In this sense, social dominance is a construct used to explain the relationship between the independent and dependent variables. Different independent variables have different strengths of effects on different dependent variables.

14. Essence of dominance

Drews (1993), proposes the following definition for dominance:

Dominance is an attribute of the pattern of repeated, agonistic interactions between two individuals, characterized by a consistent outcome in favor of the same dyad member and default yielding response of its opponent rather than escalation. The status of the consistent winner is dominant and that of the loser subordinate.

Operationally, dominance ranks (i.e., the position of one individual in a dominance hierarchy) are calculated after assessment of dominance status (the status of one individual within a dyad based on directionality of statistically significant outcomes) in every possible dyad in the group.

Drews (1993) points out that this definition is merely a structural descriptive model that allows for future study of the phenomenon. He explains that one can use the definition in order to suggest that dominance is merely a descriptive tool, an illustration of one attribute of dyadic relationships, and a useful estimate of an individual's ability to influence the behavior of others through their ability to inflict costs on others. It is a basis for explaining conventional tactics that result in the replacement of escalated aggression with avoidance or display, and to consider social dominance a product of cost–benefit considerations.

15. Formal dominance

The notion of formal dominance originated with de Waal (1986) and has since been elaborated upon by Preuschoft and van Schaik (2000). Here, I outline the contributions of both.

The directionality of communication signals, as opposed to outcomes of aggressive encounters, is highly stable across time and is hence predictable. De Waal agrees with Rowell (1966) that submissive signals are particularly consistent in their directionality, as contrasted with dominant or aggressive outcomes. Given this, de Waal argues that social dominance should really represent the directionality of signals. De Waal's (1986) "formal dominance" is a departure from the usual notion of either determining dominance based on the outcomes of agonistic contests or relating the independent variables of traits with the dependent variables of outcomes. De Waal points out that, usually, the proposed independent and dependent variables cannot be correlated well. This is the impetus for his formal dominance notion, which, rather than focusing on outcomes or these correlations, focuses solely on the independent variables.

Preuschoft and van Schaik (2000) define dominance slightly differently than in formal dominance ("long-term dyadic relationships that are characterized by an asymmetric distribution of power," p. 78), but they also focus on communication signals. They propose that "dominance in groups seems to function as a conflict management device, preventing escalated competition by conventionalizing means and priority of access, thus allowing for peaceful coexistence of group members" (p. 90).

Preuschoft and van Schaik (2000, p. 78) suggest that dominance emerges only in individuals who use contest competition, which they define as a situation in which an individual attempts to monopolize a resource. In contest competition, (a) A enhances his own interests at a cost to B, (b) A's behavior is goal directed, and (c) B is forced to incur a cost by A. This is contrasted with scramble competition, in which individuals maximize efficiency in locating and exploiting a resource so that they may consume as much as possible. In scramble competition, aggressive or other agonistic behaviors are not observed. Only in contest competitive scenarios is social dominance said to be able to emerge, since aggressive encounters and communication are likely.

This notion predicts that, as familiarity increases, escalation decreases in favor of conventional behaviors such as display and preemptive deference. It also predicts that animals will prefer to interact with familiar individuals because conventional interactions are less costly than dealing with strangers and performing full stepwise escalation and assessment; it saves time and energy.

Preuschoft and van Schaik (2000, p. 79) identify three factors that determine whether conflict results in escalated aggression: the value of the resource to each individual (and hence each individual's motivation), an estimation on the part of each individual as to how likely they are to win, and the cost each individual is willing to incur in seeking the resource. Preuschoft and van Schaik hypothesize that individuals will seek to predict the costs and benefits of competitive encounters. They suggest that individuals will initiate a stepwise escalation upon meeting in order to perform an assessment of the opponent's fighting ability in comparison to their own. This predicts that, if one individual determines through their initial assessment that they are weaker, less motivated or prepared to incur fewer costs, then they should withdraw and defer. The notion then explains that extensive assessment may become too expensive and so general rules may develop. Preuschoft and van Schaik suggest rules for different grouping patterns, but the one that concerns us here is the stable association grouping class, in which members are familiar with one another through frequent encounters. In such social relationships, prior experience with the opponent informs the decision rules, and transient behavioral signals are used. The notion proposes that prevention of escalation is a mutual interest and so signaling of fighting ability (display) can be used in place of actual escalation when the outcome is predictable. Ritualized display of fighting ability and motivation are used to inform the members of these predictable outcomes.

After repeated display and assessment interactions, in which each individual performs stepwise escalations and signaling of agonistic abilities and intentions, each can settle into conventional low-cost behaviors. Dominance–subordination relationships represent these conventional interactions. Each subsequent interaction after the first meeting adds data to each member's assessment and to their ability to predict their relative likelihood of winning an escalated contest; the power asymmetries are known.

Preuschoft and van Schaik refer to submission as an advertised harmlessness and explain that this effectively appeases the opponent and inhibits their aggression. They explain that submission acts in stable social relationships as a compensation for the dispersal effects (individuals breaking from the group and going out on their own) of competition and escalated aggression.

In terms of group structure, Preuschoft and van Schaik (2000) explain that these dyadic dominance–subordination relationships interconnect to form networks or relationships, which we refer to as dominance hierarchies. They suggest that these hierarchies can be linear (i.e., A > B > C > D > E > F), nonlinear/triangular (e.g., A > B and B > C, but C > A), pyramidal (e.g., A > [B = C = D = F]) or reflect a class system (e.g., [A + B] > [C = D + E + F]). In this way, the model allows for a variety of group structures and introduces the possibility of nondyadic relationships such as alliances and coalitions.

16. "Hawk–dove game"

The "hawk–dove game" suggests that "animals with the capacity to wreak havoc on other members of their species frequently refrain from doing so" (Barash, 2003, p. 216) and asks the question "how are we to explain those wonderful, fascinating cases of restrained lethality" (Barash, 2003, p. 216) from an evolutionary standpoint? John Maynard Smith and George Price (as discussed in

Barash, 2003, p. 217) attempted to answer that question with a game theoretic model of the evolution of social conflict called the hawk–dove game.

In the hawk–dove game, there are two types of individuals: hawks and doves. Each type represents a different strategy. The hawk threatens and then, if necessary, they fight. The dove avoids escalated aggression. The hawk–dove game aims to explain how these two basic behavioral strategies might coexist in the same group at the same time. As with all strategic games, a matrix can be formed in which the payoffs for the combinations of dyadic strategies are outlined. The matrix for the hawk–dove game is illustrated below.

	Dove	Hawk
Dove	1/2(v – c), 1/2(v – c)	v,0
Hawk	0,v	1/2v, 1/2v

Table 1. Payoff matrix for basic hawk–dove game, where c represents cost and v represents value. In each of the four quadrants, the figures before the comma represent the payoff for player #1 and the figures after the comma represent the payoff for player #2. Player 1 is the vertical axis, or the rows; Player 2 is the horizontal axis, or the columns.

This payoff matrix identifies the costs c and value v (measured in units of reproductive fitness) faced by players who may use these basic strategies in a contest for a limited resource. If each individual is a hawk, he or she will fight until one individual is seriously injured, and the winner will possess and consume the resource in question. Each individual is equally likely to win, which makes this a symmetric game. If both individuals play dove, then each consumes the resource with a probability of 1/2, without a fight (Osborne, 2004, p. 398). The strategy set (hawk, hawk) is a unique Nash equilibrium (a strategy profile in which no player has an alternative strategy that increases their payoff, given the other players' strategy) and hence hawk is an evolutionarily stable action if $v > c$. If $v = c$, then hawk–hawk is an equilibrium also, but not a strict one. If $v < c$, then the game has no symmetric Nash equilibrium with pure strategies (Osborne, 2004, pp. 399–400). If hawks are abundant, they gain a higher payoff, but as they become more abundant, they face more hawks in their contests and their payoffs begin to suffer relative to the dove strategy. At this point, the dove strategy becomes favorable. However, as the doves then increase in frequency, they become vulnerable to invasion by hawks. Neither strategy, on its own, is evolutionarily stable. If the cost of fighting increases, the proportion of hawks at equilibrium decreases. If the value of the resource increases, then the proportion of hawks should also increase.

The above focuses on pure strategies, in which the players choose either the hawk or dove strategy alone. A mixed strategy would allow the player to choose which of the two strategies they will employ, based on a probability. Maynard Smith and Price inserted the values 10 for value of resource, 20 for the cost of fighting in hawks, and 3 as the cost of wasted time displaying in doves. With these arbitrary values, it can be determined that hawks make up 8/13 of the population and doves make up 5/13 of the population (Barash, 2003, p. 219). Rather than there being 8 hawks and 5 doves in a population of 13 members, each member could change their strategy from hawk to dove or vice versa, with a probability of 8/13 playing hawk and 5/13 playing dove.

A variant of the hawk–dove game can transform it into an asymmetric contest.

	Dove	Hawk
Dove	1/2V, 1/2v	0, v
Hawk	V, 0	1/2 (V − c), 1/2 (v − c)

Table 2. Variant of the hawk–dove game with asymmetry. V is the value of the resource (territory) to the owner, v is the value of the resource (territory) to the intruder and c represents the cost.

In this case, the rows are player 1, who is the owner of a territory, and the columns are player 2, who is the intruder. Strategies hawk–dove and dove–hawk are equilibrium strategies if V < c and v < c. The strategy in which the intruder defers to the owner is called the bourgeois strategy and is common in the animal kingdom. The strategy in which the owner defers to the intruder is not common at all and is called the paradoxical strategy (Osborne, 2004, p. 409).

17. "War-of-attrition model"

The "war-of-attrition model" is a game theoretic representation of two animals fighting over a prey resource, but it can model many other disputes; the prey could represent any indivisible resource, and fighting can represent any costly behavior (including mere waiting).

In the war-of-attrition model, each competitor determines a point in time during a contest at which they will concede if their opponent has not already conceded. The competitor who is prepared to endure the longest in the contest will consume the resource and the other will not. Duration of enduring is related to the cost the individual is prepared to incur in order to consume the resource. In the war-of-attrition model, time is considered continuous rather than discrete, starts with zero and runs indefinitely. It is assumed that the value player i assigns to the resource is $v_i > 0$. The value they assign to a 50% probability of consuming the resource is $v_i/2$. The dispute is settled when one of the competitors concedes. The cost of enduring for one unit of time is considered one unit. For example, if i concedes first at t_i, her payoff is $-t_i$. On the other hand, if the other player j concedes first at time unit t_j, player i's payoff would be $v_i - t_j$. The third possible outcome is for each opponent to concede at the same time, in which case i's payoff would be $1/2 v_i - t_i$ (Osborne, 2004, p. 77).

18. Parker's model of escalated fighting and resource holding power (RHP)

The notion of resource holding power (RHP) is a measure of absolute fighting ability of an individual. It is part of a model of escalation of aggression in competitive encounters (Parker, 1974).

The model asks the question: how should the outcomes of aggressive disputes during a fight be decided? The answer Parker (1974) offers is that each individual possesses a fitness budget. When an opponent inflicts an injury upon an individual, their fitness budget declines. Through mutual assessment, each opponent estimates which should run out of this fitness budget first. The one that should deplete their fitness budget first should defer before escalation occurs.

Parker (1974) points out that, with equal RHPs, there might be circumstances in which payoff imbalances exist. Whether an individual is the holder of a resource or the attacking intruder is one such case, whereby the possessor will have a higher RHP than the intruder, even if otherwise they would be equal. In the case of a resource holder versus an attacker, the attacker will have to possess a significantly greater fitness budget in order to surpass the holder advantage.

Each opponent in a conflict assesses the relative RHP, which correlates to an absolute probability (cacb) of winning the next bout. A bout is determined by the infliction of an injury. Each individual spends from their fitness budget in order to inflict injury on their opponent and for their withdrawal. This defines the critical probability (ccrit) of winning the next bout for each opponent. If cabs > ccrit, escalation is the better strategy. If cabs < ccrit, withdrawal is the better strategy.

Parker explains that assessment of RHP is an evolutionarily stable strategy (ESS) because any individuals choosing a different strategy would fail to defer to individuals with higher RHP, fail to gain the resource in question, suffer injury, and become less likely to reproduce. The strategy of assessing RHP and using assessment before choosing whether to escalate (limited war) is assumed to be an ESS over total war and total peace. If the opponent escalates, then escalating after conventional assessment is attempted is the preferred strategy.

The model suggests that those individuals who respond to RHP thresholds appropriately before they withdraw will be selected for. Parker (1974) describes it this way: "given that his RHP is x and mine is y, and that in this situation I have a units available to expend and he has b units, will I run out of expendable fitness units before he does?"

Parker (1974) lays out his main model in five points:

The function of conventional fighting (display) is to allow each individual to assess their opponent's relative RHP, providing an absolute probability (cabs) for each combatant to win the first bout in an escalated fight. A bout is determined by the infliction of an injury upon an opponent. The probability of winning (cabs) is assumed to be directly proportional to the relation between the individuals' respective RHPs. Where x and y are individuals, this is stated rx/(rx + ry).

"Suppose that the loss in fitness due to an injury in the first bout would be 1. For this possible loss, there will be a critical minimum probability of winning the first bout (ccrit) below which retreat (rather than escalation) is the more favorable strategy. ccrit is greater the greater the search cost for an alternative resource."

If and only if cabs > ccrit for both individuals, then escalation is expected to occur. If cabs > ccrit for one individual and cabs < ccrit for another, then the latter is expected to defer or disengage rather than face the loss of fitness likely in the conflict. If cabs < ccrit for both individuals, then the winner is expected to be the one with the lesser negative score.

After the first bout, each combatant will reassess. As a result, of the outcome of the first bout, the loser's RHP and cabs will decrease, while the winner's cabs will increase. This is consistent with observations of losers disengaging after damaging bouts in conflict encounters.

The goal of the "game" is to "play" for the disengagement of the opponent; for the reversal of their cabs > ccrit to cabs < ccrit.

Whether an individual will choose the withdraw strategy or the escalate strategy will depend on whether the "probable future fitness gain rate due to continued investment in the resource (in gain extraction, fighting, courtship persistence, etc.)" is greater or less than the "probable future fitness gain due to withdrawal for resumption of searching for alternative resources."

Analysis

Each of the 18 notions of social dominance was systematically analyzed as outlined above. The results are summarized in Table 3.

1. Privileged role dominance

"Privileged role dominance" was determined to be a connotative definition. Although this definition requires two or more individuals in at least two encounters, it does not require that previous encounters affect the outcome of future encounters. Neither Drews (1993) nor Wilson (1975) state or imply that previous encounters affect future encounters. Therefore, I discarded this definition because it failed the social relationship criterion.

2. Reproductive dominance

"Reproductive dominance" was determined to be an explanation. This explanation requires neither that previous encounters affect future encounters nor that two individuals meet at least two times. I discarded this explanation because it failed the social relationship criterion.

3. Dominance is aggressiveness

"Dominance is aggressiveness" provides an explanation. Although this explanation requires two or more individuals in at least two encounters, it does not require that previous encounters affect the outcome of future encounters. Therefore, this explanation failed the social relationship criterion and was discarded.

4. Dominance is a trait that conveys rank

"Dominance is a trait that conveys rank" was determined to be an explanation. Although this explanation requires two or more individuals in at least two encounters, it does not require that previous encounters affect the outcome of future encounters. Therefore, I discarded this explanation because it failed the social relationship criterion.

5. Winner is dominant, loser is subordinate

"Winner is dominant, loser is subordinate" was determined to be a connotative definition. This definition neither requires that previous encounters affect future encounters nor that two individuals meet at least two times. Therefore, I discarded this explanation because it failed the social relationship criterion.

6. Successful combatant

"Successful combatant" was determined to be an explanation. This explanation neither requires that previous encounters affect future encounters nor that two individuals meet at least two times. I discarded this explanation because it failed the social relationship criterion.

7. Dominance is lack of aggressiveness

"Dominance is lack of aggressiveness" was determined to be an explanation. This explanation neither requires that previous encounters affect future encounters nor that two individuals meet at least two times.

8. Consistent winner of agonistic contests

"Consistent winner of agonistic contests" was determined to be a connotative definition. Although this definition requires two or more individuals in at least two encounters, it does not require that previous encounters affect the outcome of future encounters. Therefore, I discarded this definition because it failed the social relationship criterion.

9. Spheres of dominance

"Spheres of dominance" provides both a connotative definition and an explanation. I retained this definition and explanation because they met the social relationship criterion.

Definition analysis

I specifically considered Hand's (1986) compound definition for social dominance (as "consistent winning at points of social conflict, regardless of the tactics used...." and "refers specifically to 'familiar' dyads in which one party follows the 'rule' that it will defer"). I retained Hand's definition for social dominance because it fell within an acceptable range and met the connotative definition criteria, but it suffers slightly from ambiguous terminology (e.g., "familiarity") and from being slightly narrow (e.g., requiring that one member of a dyad follow the rule that they will defer).

Explanation analysis

It is important to note that Hand's explanation for dominance is based specifically on his definition of dominance and not on his definition of social dominance. I would have discarded this definition for dominance because it would not have met the social relationship criterion. However, because he also provided a definition of social dominance, I assessed that. I retained the explanation because it met each of the explanation analysis criteria.

Definition value

Hand's definition of social dominance puts "familiar" and "rule" in full quotes, indicating that he realizes that these terms might be vague or ambiguous. However, he defines "rule" in the same sentence as meaning "deferring," so that is redeemed. The term "familiar" is defined by onelook.com this way: "adjective: having mutual interests or affections; of established friendship (Example: 'On familiar terms'); adjective: well known or easily recognized (Example: 'A familiar figure'); adjective: within normal everyday experience; common and ordinary; not strange" (onelook.com, n.d.), which is consistent with everyday use of the term. Clearly, "familiar" refers to relationships in which the individuals meet repeatedly and remember each other.

Another potential source of vagueness is the statement that one party follows the rule. Hand does not state whether it has to be only one individual to follow the rule or whether the two individuals can alternate in following the rule. He does state that only one party follows the rule, but does this mean that only one party follows the rule within the encounters they share or that each party takes turns following the rule? My interpretation of this is that " 'familiar' dyads in which one party follows the 'rule' that it will defer" means that one, and only one, member of the "familiar dyad" follows this rule. If the definition had stated that within a particular encounter one member follows the rule, I would tend to interpret this as allowing for alternate rule following. But because the topic is the relationship rather than one particular encounter, it seems logical that the statement "follows the rule" should apply consistently to the topic, which is the relationship as a whole. For these reasons, I have determined that "one party follows the rule" means that one, and only one, party within a dyadic relationship always follows the rule. If I am wrong in my interpretation, then I would argue that the definition is vague, in which case I would not have retained it beyond the definition analysis criteria stage.

Given the resolution of potential vagaries within the definition, I can discuss the limits of inclusion. This definition would describe all situations involving social relationships in which encounters resolve by one member always deferring. The definition allows for any means by which this may come about (including force options or leverage). It can refer to any encounter in which the subordinate preemptively defers, as well as situations in which display behaviors are exchanged, or when escalated aggression takes place, or even when one defers because the other has some form of leverage over them.

This definition would exclude any nonsocial relationships, as well as any social encounters in which it is not one particular member that defers each time. If the other member sometimes defers, this definition would no longer consider it a case of social dominance. In that case, it would seem this definition no longer considers this "consistent winning."

The value of this definition is severely limited because it excludes social relationships in which the same dyad member is not always the one who defers. It does address the observation that in dominance relationships there usually is a consistent asymmetry in the outcomes of agonistic encounters, but it is too severe in ruling out all cases except ones in which one particular member always defers.

Overall, this definition is of moderate value.

Explanation value

Hand raises a number of unique, and potentially very useful, notions in his explanation of how social dominance operates. One of the ideas is that social dominance may be contextual; that is, an individual may be dominant in one context but not in others. This might help explain why there is such poor correlation between contexts and outcomes in studies of conflict. For example, we know that in wolves the male is dominant in such matters as food but the female is often dominant in matters of rearing of young (Mech, 1999). By postulating spheres of dominance, we explain these seeming irregularities. Of course, this might make the hypothesis difficult to test in many cases, and it comes with the risk of circularity or begging-the-question problems. For example, if we leave open the possibility of identifying any time an individual in a dyad wins as a context and any time his opponent wins as another context, we have a problem. Of course, if we make sure that winning in that context remains stable across time, then we escape this difficulty. Furthermore, if we identify specific rational categories of contexts prior to testing hypotheses about their stability, we can also escape this problem. If we allow for spheres of dominance, they must be stable across time in previously specified contexts in order to be useful.

Another unusual aspect of the "spheres of dominance" explanation is that it proposes that social dominance resolves many kinds of social conflict and not just those involving resources. Conventionally, we think of social dominance as related solely to the resolution of conflict over resources, but Hand (1986) points out that, too often, reference to dominance as defined by access to resources is circular (dominance is access to resources and those who get access to resources are dominant). Hand identifies various social conflicts that are not about resources, yet are moderated by the dominance/subordinate relationship. The "spheres of dominance" explanation helps us encompass these, along with access to resources, as affected by social dominance. This helps us explain such social conflicts as decisions about the direction a troop of primates will travel or which gull will be allowed to sit and incubate the eggs. Other explanations of social dominance related solely to priority of access to resources exclude these cases.

Hand also distinguishes social dominance from egalitarian systems and unresolved relationships. By doing this, the "spheres of dominance" explanation does not force all agonistic encounters into a dominance framework. This is particularly useful in helping us explain various patterns we observe in social structures, such as consistent winning versus relatively equal winning versus relationships which are as yet unresolved (in that an individual wins and loses in rapid succession).

Overall, the "spheres of dominance" model helps us understand issues surrounding contextual differences in outcomes of social conflict situations, and what social dominance is as contrasted with aggressive dominance and egalitarian systems of social structure. This model is wide reaching and perhaps the most valuable of the explanations retained to the value assessment stage. All considered, I would rate this model at the high end of a moderate value.

10. Priority of access to resources

"Priority of access to resources" was determined to be a connotative definition. Although this definition requires previous encounters to affect the outcome of future encounters, it does not require two or more individuals in at least two encounters. Therefore, I discarded this definition because it failed the social relationship criterion.

11. Peck order

"Peck order" was determined to be a connotative definition. This definition requires that previous encounters affect future encounters, and that two individuals meet at least two times. I retained this definition because it meets the social relationship criterion and all of the connotative definition criteria. This definition is not operationally identical to any other definition retained to this stage of analysis.

Definition value

The "peck order" definition is limited because it identifies "pecking" as the necessary type of agonistic encounter. Applied to chickens, particularly chickens kept in crowded and contrived conditions, this definition allows us to identify the dominant from the subordinate within a dyad and hence allows us to formulate a hierarchy of social dominance rank. If this social structure remains stable across time, then this might be of value in determining rank within these crowded chicken populations, but it does not allow us, on the face of it, to apply the term dominance to other species that do not peck.

If we assume (for sake of argument) that the word peck could be replaced with the idea that any agonistic attack type could be used, the definition becomes much more useful. In that case, we could look at social relationships and determine whether a social dominance system is present by observing the directionality of agonistic attack behaviors. This sets up a rather extreme criterion for inclusion because it is likely that, in some social groups, attacks occur in both directions rather than in just one direction. Under this definition, anything short of 100% in one direction is excluded from being referred to as social dominance. The definition was nevertheless defined clearly.

The definition does not account for preemptive deference. In many cases, which we might like to refer to as social dominance, a subordinate might defer prior to being attacked. We might like to see this as an interaction involving a dominant and subordinate, but if no "pecks" take place, we are unable to define the situation as involving social dominance. The neglect of preemptive deference limits this definition even further.

Generally speaking, this definition is clear but quite limited in its applicability and value because it makes use of pecking specifically rather than any other agonistic behaviors; it sets up an extreme criterion for membership by excluding all cases that are less than 100% unidirectional, and it does not account for preemptive deference. Therefore, I would rate this definition as of low value.

12. Barrette and Vandal's dominance

"Barrette and Vandal's dominance" provides both a connotative definition and explanation. Although this definition requires previous encounters to affect the outcome of future encounters, it does not require two or more individuals in at least two encounters. I discarded this definition, and also the explanation because it failed the social relationship criterion.

Explanation analysis

The hypothesis states that social structure is a function of differences in outcomes of agonistic encounters, deference, and history of past relationship. Although this explanation requires that previous encounters affect future encounters, and that two individuals meet, it does not require that the individuals meet at least two times. Barrette and Vandal do not state whether dominance requires more than one encounter, but they do state that for ranking of individuals within a group "...the observer has ideally recorded at least one interaction in all the dyads in the group." Barrette and Vandal go on to outline their study, in which they determine rank in cases of single encounters. While this explanation certainly allows for social relationships, it does not require them. Therefore, it was appropriate to discard this explanation because it failed the social relationship criterion.

13. Intervening variable

The "intervening variable" was determined to be an explanation. This explanation requires at least two individuals to encounter one another in at least two encounters, and it requires that previous encounters affect the outcome of future encounters. Therefore, this explanation meets the social relationship criterion.

Explanation analysis

This explanation satisfied all of the explanation criteria and was retained for value assessment. It is not operationally identical to any other explanation retained to this stage of analysis.

Explanation value

The "intervening variable" explanation is a special case, because the focus of the explanation is an attempt to clarify the type of model used to understand the phenomenon of social dominance. As reviewed above, the intervening variable explanation suggests that social dominance is best not considered a dependent variable or independent variable but rather an intervening variable, much as "intelligence" is. The authors also suggest that there may be interaction between independent variables that results in social dominance. In this regard, the intervening variable explanation helps explain one major problem in the field of social dominance: disappointing intercorrelation among independent variables. In other words, the various factors that result in particular outcomes of agonistic encounters are generally not well correlated with one another. This has been a major drawback of theories of social dominance, which have attempted to describe these factors. The proposal that social dominance is an intervening variable and that the independent variables involved have interacting relationships explains why correlations have been weak (if social dominance reflects a real phenomenon). What we need now is a model that would identify these interacting relationships. This is a promising avenue in research. In that limited sense, the "intervening variable" explanation is moderately valuable.

In their article, Hinde and Datta (1981) propose certain independent variables and their relative strength of influence upon the intervening variable of dominance, and the relative strength of influence of dominance upon their proposed dependent variables.

This explanation may help explain any phenomena that must relate common relationship features with the observed behaviors constituting outcomes. For example, if we observe A supplanting B, this model suggests that size, maternal rank, hormonal condition and dyadic experience are most influential, and that age is less influential, on putative outcome. Likewise, if we observe that A has priority of access to resources over B, then we expect this to be influenced to a lesser extent by size, maternal rank, hormonal condition and dyadic experience than when A supplants B. It is influenced more by age.

What determines whether B is submissive toward A? This model proposes that size, maternal rank, hormonal condition, dyadic experience and age are relevant factors. The model generates specific and testable hypotheses, which is a major asset.

It may be that this explanation is more relevant to certain primate societies than other species, and that specific independent and dependent variables, and their relative strength of influence, must be identified for different species. Maternal rank, grooming and leading (i.e., walking first and determining direction of travel) are particularly important in certain primate societies and less prominent in other species. The explanatory power of the model is greater than would otherwise be the case, to the extent that it is shown to be consistent with empirical evidence for certain species and less consistent with other species. It would still be valuable to have a framework for devising these kinds of species-specific models, and this is what the intervening variable model offers. It would also be extremely valuable to identify within this framework any independent and dependent variables and their relative strengths of influence broadly across species.

. Size, maternal rank, hormonal condition, dyadic experience and age, but not experience of the terrain, affect dominance, whereas age and experience of the terrain and—to a lesser extent—size, maternal rank, hormonal condition and dyadic experience influence authority most prominently. Dominance results in outcome-observations, such as A supplanting B, B grooming A, B submitting to A and, to a lesser extent, A having priority of access to resources, but not to A leading while B follows. Authority leads to the observations of A having priority of access to resources and, to a greater extent, A leading and B following.

Extensive empirical study will be required to devise well-tested models within this intervening variable framework. Potentially, variables and the relationships between them would have to be identified for each species under consideration.

14. *Essence of dominance*

"Essence of dominance" was determined to be a connotative definition. Although this definition requires two or more individuals in at least two encounters, it does not require that previous encounters affect the outcome of future encounters.

Therefore, I discarded this definition because it failed the social relationship criterion.

15. Formal dominance

"Formal dominance" provides both a connotative definition and explanation. Both the definition and explanation require at least two individuals to encounter one another in at least two encounters, and they require that previous encounters affect the outcome of future encounters. Therefore, I retained both the definition and explanation because they meet the social relationship criterion.

This definition is not operationally identical to any other connotative definition retained to this stage of analysis, and the explanation is not operationally identical to any other explanation retained to this stage of analysis.

Definition analysis

The "formal dominance" definition meets each of the connotative definition criteria except the "ambiguous, obscure, or figurative language" criterion. The "formal dominance" definition uses two terms that are less clear than they should be. "Long term" and "power" are vague, making this definition far less useful than some other definitions. Long term means "relating to or affecting a time long into the future" (encarta.msn.com, n.d.), which could, even in reasonable scale, mean days, weeks, months, or years. Unless the authors define the timeframe intended, I simply do not know the intention of the definition. Power can mean "possession of controlling influence... one possessing or exercising power or influence or authority... possession of the qualities (especially mental qualities) required to do something or get something... physical strength" (onelook.com1, n.d.). Does the definition refer to physical strength? Might it perhaps refer to one of the other descriptions above, each of which is rather vague in themselves, in this context? Without a more specific notion of what these two terms mean, it is impossible to evaluate it. Consequently, I discarded this definition.

Explanation analysis

I retained for value assessment the "formal dominance" explanation because it met each of the explanation criteria.

Explanation value

The "formal dominance" explanation seems reasonable, but it focuses on communication signals as an indication of dominance. The authors state that these cannot be correlated with outcomes, and so I cannot see what "signal direction" really tells us. Since the explanation does not claim to be able to correlate outcomes with communication signals—and in fact they point to this as a reason for using communication signals—the "formal dominance" explanation was not discarded at the explanation analysis stage, but this certainly is a confusing aspect of this explanation.

De Waal's (1986, 2000) contribution to "formal dominance" is to explain social dominance as related to the directionality of communication signals between individuals in social relationships, as opposed to explaining social dominance by way of the outcomes of agonistic encounters.

This in itself is of limited value because de Waal's "formal dominance" does not explain the relationship between directionality of communication signals and dominance (the exertion of control over others). If this explanation avoids the problem of intercorrelation of outcomes and traits, then what does directionality of communication signals tell us except that communication signals themselves are unidirectional? Of what use is knowing the directionality of signals if it does not allow us to predict outcomes, particularly regarding the exertion of influence or control? It would seem that identifying unidirectional communication signals independent of outcomes would be of far less value than an explanation of social dominance that explains resource allocation (i.e., outcomes).

Preuschoft and van Schaik's (2000) contribution to this focus on communication was to provide a better framework for de Waal's ideas. They explain why social dominance has evolved: "dominance in groups seems to function as a conflict management device, preventing escalated competition by conventionalizing means and priority of access, thus allowing for peaceful coexistence of group members" (p. 90). They also explain how social dominance operates, by identifying three factors that determine whether conflict results in escalated aggression: the value of the resource to each individual (and hence each individual's motivation), an estimation on the part of each individual as to how likely they are to win, and the cost each individual is willing to incur in seeking the resource (p. 79).

"Formal dominance," consequently, explains how and why overt aggression is replaced with conventional behaviors such as display of intent and fighting ability within social relationships. This element was neglected in the "Barrette and Vandal's dominance" definition explored above. "Formal dominance" also explains why replacement of overt aggression by conventional behaviors occurs in a gradual process (because a stepwise assessment of display behavior is required in order for each member to learn the costs and benefits involved in escalating). "Formal dominance" also explains how and why some individuals in social relationships will preemptively defer to others in situations of contested resources. When we observe the various relationships between dyadic relationships within a society, "formal dominance" explains the different classes of structure we measure (i.e., linear, nonlinear, and pyramidal).

In the field of psychology, social dominance can help us explain the interactions of humans in families, in the workplace, and in other groups of at least two people in which repeated encounters take place. In situations in which resources are limited and competition within these stable groups occurs, social dominance is predicted to take place. The "formal dominance" notion explains why it develops and how it operates.

"Formal dominance" predicts how behavior changes through time, and that communication signals will develop called submissive signals and/or dominance signals. The submissive signals are predicted to be extremely stable and unidirectional. They indicate that the sender advertises their lack of intention to actively compete for the resource in question. Dominance behaviors are also said to be stable and unidirectional, indicating a reinforcement of the sender's intention to actively compete for the resource. Examples of submissive behaviors that might be seen in humans in family or work groups might include failure to make eye contact, disengaging from a confrontation, and other signals that the sender uses to endear themselves to the other and otherwise indicate that they do not intend to escalate. By doing so, they advertise that there is no need for the dominant individual to make use of overt aggression or other leverage acts to reinforce their preferential access to the resource.

In biology, "formal dominance" helps explain why we see similar communication signals in stable social relationships. In groups that form social relationships, such as wolves, we observe directional communication signals, reduction of overt aggression over time in relationships, replacement of overt aggression with conventional behavior and other social interactions described by the "formal dominance" explanation.

An extremely wide variety of important social interactions occurs between both humans and nonhumans, and "formal dominance" accounts for many of the observations common to these interactions. I would rate this explanation at the high end of moderate value.

16. Hawk–dove game

The "hawk–dove game" was determined to be an explanation. This explanation requires at least two interacting individuals in at least two encounters, and requires that previous encounters affect the outcome of future encounters. Therefore, this explanation met the social relationship criterion. This explanation is not operationally identical to any other explanations retained to this stage of analysis.

Explanation analysis

I retained the hawk–dove game explanation because it met each of the explanation criteria.

Explanation value

The hawk–dove game offers a unique approach to understanding why social animals would avoid conflict or escalate aggression and how such strategies could remain stable within societies. It brings a more rigorous approach to understanding these strategies.

Social dominance is what happens to social structure when asymmetries in fighting ability and other qualities exist. In that regard, the main theory of the hawk–dove game is severely limited because it models symmetric contests. The variant that introduces asymmetries is of much more value since it allows us to explore the relationship between costs and values for escalation versus disengagement in situations in which asymmetries exist. By focusing on the payoffs (both costs and benefits) of the strategies in question, the hawk–dove game makes use of a simple, important guiding principle in behavior.

The choice of strategies is also useful. The hawk strategy and the dove strategy can be thought of as the escalate/dominate strategy and the defer/submit strategy, respectively, and the payoff matrix allows for modeling of various dominance scenarios.

The theoretical framework of game theory allows us to explore various phenomena such as social dominance—indeed, anything involving decision making. By systematically matching a payoff structure to each strategy for each "player," this model helps us see why these strategies could have evolved. It also helps us predict the decision-making process for individuals. It offers a probability for the choice of available strategies for each player, which we can test empirically.

Barash (2003, p. 227) points out that game theory and the hawk–dove game are particularly useful when behavior is not so obviously related to asymmetries between players. When behavior is related to asymmetries, game theory is less useful. The hawk–dove game itself is of low value because it models symmetric relationships.

17. War-of-attrition model

The "war-of-attrition model" was determined to be an explanation. This explanation neither requires that previous encounters affect future encounters nor requires that two individuals meet at least two times. I discarded this explanation because it failed the social relationship criterion.

18. Parker's model of escalated fighting and resource holding power (RHP)

"Escalated fighting and resource holding power" was determined to be an explanation. This explanation neither requires that previous encounters affect future encounters nor that two individuals meet at least two times. I discarded this explanation because it failed the social relationship criterion.

Name of Notion	Denotative Definition	Connotative Definition	Explanation
1. Privileged role dominance		DIS	
2. Reproductive dominance			DIS
3. Dominance is aggressiveness			DIS
4. Dominance is a trait that conveys rank			DIS
5. Winner is dominant, loser is subordinate		DIS	
6. Successful combat			DIS
7. Dominance is lack of aggressiveness			DIS
8. Consistent winner of agonistic contests		DIS	
9. Spheres of dominance		MOD	MOD
10. Priority of access to resources		DIS	
11. Peck order		LOW	
12. Barrette and Vandal's dominance		DIS	DIS
13. Intervening variable			LOW
14. Essence of dominance		DIS	
15. Formal dominance		DIS	MOD
16. Hawk–dove game			LOW
17. War-of-attrition model			DIS
18. Parker's model of escalated fighting and resource holding power			DIS

Table 3. Results of analysis showing the classification of each notion and whether it survived to the value assessment stage. DIS = Discarded; LOW = Retained to value assessment and determined to be of low value; MOD = Retained to value assessment and determined to be of moderate value; HIGH = Retained to value assessment and determined to be of high value.

Discussion

I started with 18 notions of dominance, which I extracted from a review of the literature. After differentiating definitions and explanations, I established 21 distinct notions of social dominance. Two definitions and five explanations survived to the value assessment phase. I found neither definition to be particularly useful as they both were at variance with conventional notions of social dominance in some important way. I found the "spheres of dominance" definition to be more useful than the "peck order" definition.

The most valuable explanation was most likely "spheres of dominance," although "formal dominance" was also moderately useful. The game theory model brings needed rigor to the problem, but it does not bring it to exactly the problem we want to understand. The game theoretic approach does show promise as a framework for modeling social dominance.

In the present study, my goal was to address the question of what social dominance is and of what value it is, by means of a conceptually systematic approach. Because social dominance is often treated in a haphazard manner, my goal was to lay a foundation for theoretical advancement. By providing a rationale for inclusion and exclusion of notions, and by differentiating between explanations, connotative and denotative definitions, I have created a filter through which we can identify putative notions of social dominance, and a way to evaluate these notions in an appropriate manner. Definitions and explanations are best evaluated with different criteria.

In the final value assessment phase, the evaluation was qualitative. The accuracy of the evaluation will rest on one's agreement that the notion should conform to the general understanding of what a notion of social dominance should refer to and that I have made a fair determination of this. Furthermore, a determination of value is based on a scale that I also determined. It is my belief that social dominance could be a theory that would explain the social organization resulting from the exertion of influence and control within social relationships. This is an extremely broad and widely applicable field of interest. If a theory were to have such wide-reaching explanatory power, making significant predictions that would apply to all society-forming species, it would provide a large explanatory power. In order to achieve this, the notion should not merely be a good story but should also provide a theoretically strong model, conforming to established requirements for that. It is with this potential that the scale of value assessment was made. None of the notions evaluated provides this optimum potential as a theory (or even definition). A value assessment resulting in a rating of high would rightly be reserved for a theory with wide applicability, and higher explanatory and predictive power. It should also clearly state the assumptions, variables, factors and predictions in a coherent manner.

In the case of moderately rated explanations and definitions, in some cases minor adjustment could result in a higher rating. In this study, I did not attempt to modify the notions or systematically tease out valuable aspects of them. This will likely be a very important step in gaining greater clarity of the topic and eventually coming to agreement on more valuable, formal notions of social dominance.

Certain common features of notions of social dominance presented themselves throughout this study. Some features were exposed as problematic or flawed, while others are likely to be important in a proper model of social dominance. Here I would like to discuss some of these important features as a way to stimulate further theory development.

Social dominance seems to function as a conflict resolution mechanism that regulates overt aggression. Most fundamentally, social dominance is a construct we use to describe the observed pattern in social relationships, which seems to allow members of societies to exert influence and control over others in competitive encounters for limited resources, while minimizing the risks associated with overt aggression. It is observed that animals in societies are less aggressive with one another than they are toward intruders invading their territories. It is also observed that the more potentially damaging the weaponry of the individuals, the more obvious is social dominance. It is also observed that, when groups of individuals are forced into crowded conditions, social dominance systems arise where they were not so pronounced before. These observations can be explained by naming the organizational patterns or mechanisms observed "social dominance" and hypothesizing that their function is to reduce the risks associated with overt aggression.

Depending on how broadly we wish to define resources, we might consider all objectives contested for as resources. Some objectives that individuals compete for may not be thought by some to be resources. For example, access to a mate or the opportunity to literally lead a troop may be considered resources. With a broad definition of resources, competition among social animals might be considered always related to resources.

Hand (1986) argues that leverage can be used to maintain resource allocation and competitive advantage as well as overt aggression. By considering leverage, we significantly improve the power of the model.

A key component of a model of social dominance should probably involve the idea that individuals will make use of a cost–benefit evaluation in determining their strategies and tactics for competitive encounters. There may be many risks associated with competition for resources within a society. The risks of being harmed or expending energy in a contest are important in a society, and so too might be damage to social relationships and loss of social group cohesion, an important asset in society-forming species. The benefits include access to the resource itself and may include a reputation factor, whereby opponents learn to defer in future encounters. This would significantly improve the economics of social living in future encounters. Of course, benefits and risks will be related to motivating operations such as satiation or deprivation. We would expect that a deprived individual would be more likely to perceive the resource as worth a higher risk than a satiated individual. This might explain why dominant individuals frequently yield access to a resource to a subordinate.

Information based on previous experience (learning) is important in determining a course of action. This information could come from at least two different sources. One source of information is from the outcomes of previous encounters with the same opponent. Another is information from experience with individuals who share some characteristics of relevance with the opponent. Consistently losing to a particular opponent in the past would tend to indicate a greater risk and a lesser opportunity for benefit. This individual is more likely (all else equal) to defer rather than escalate. Conversely, consistent winning in such a situation would lead to a lesser likelihood of deferring.

Another element that might be factored into a model of social dominance is temperamental disposition to assertiveness. Assertiveness is a variable general behavior trait within a population, and it seems reasonable to assume that the more assertive will be more likely to exert power and influence over others.

How might we put such factors to work in a model of social dominance? Each encounter could result in decisions based on the factors discussed above or others in various ways. When we talk about decisions, we are in a position to make use of game theory. This cost–benefit evaluation can be represented in a game theory payoff matrix to utilize the benefits of that approach. An iterated game theoretic model would help us explore in simulation studies the various parameters through many interactions or even generations.

Further research needs to be carried out in which formal, complete and coherent models of social dominance are proposed. Mathematical approaches or logical argumentation would be valuable approaches to formalizing some of the weak notions that lack clarity. Once formal models have been articulated, my next suggestion is computer simulation. This would allow for extensive exploration of the models. By doing computer simulation studies with formal models, each parameter can be explored in detail across thousands of encounters and even thousands of generations. Finally, of course, predictions that the models generate should be compared with empirical data to determine the usefulness of the model. Studies founded on vague or weak theoretical bases provide us with vague and weak evidence. Only with a strong, clear theoretical basis can empirical studies provide evidence that will help us gain useful insights into the structure of social relationships and group dynamics.

The notion of social dominance will probably be more useful in some contexts than others. It promises to be useful in an ethological / sociological context as an explanation for various observations, although there are other, more behavioral, models that may be at least as useful, if not more so. In the context of explaining, predicting and, most importantly, changing companion animal behavior, social dominance offers little help. In the history of its use and misuse in the context of explaining and changing companion animal behavior, it has been used to promote, explicitly or implicitly, an adversarial relationship between human and companion animal, which has resulted in degradation of the social bond and precipitous decline in the animal's welfare. It has also been used to promote abusive treatment of companion animals. In the context of companion animal behavior, social dominance seems to have done far more harm than good.

Conclusion

What is social dominance? Based on the value assessment of the surviving notions, social dominance is a construct describing features of a social relationship that addresses the resolution of social conflict, including but not limited to the allocation of limited resources, through the exertion of control and influence. This takes place in a way that minimizes the risk of overt aggression by way of the use of conventionalized display behaviors. This minimization of risk involves a cost–benefit evaluation of the benefits of seeking to win a particular social conflict versus the likely associated cost. The term "exertion of control and influence" means the involvement of aggressive behavior and/or other forms of leverage. I differentiate social dominance from other forms of dominance by its occurrence in social relationships. "Social" in the context of the term social dominance refers to the quality of a series of at least two encounters between at least two individuals such that the information remembered from previous social encounters with that particular individual affects future encounters.

Of what value are the available notions of social dominance? Potentially, social dominance could be very valuable in an ethological and social psychological context because it helps us understand the dynamics of competitive encounters and exertion of power in social relationships. This is useful in a wide variety of fields within psychology and biology. The notion of social dominance could help us understand why animals in social relationships avoid overt aggression and how this mechanism operates. It would allow us to predict the course of social relationships in society-forming species as a sociological and ethological construct. It might even help us understand better why we and some other species are social. Each of these is an incredibly important field of inquiry. As it stands, the value of present notions of social dominance is at best disappointingly moderate in comparison with this ideal. The reason I reach this conclusion is a general lack of rigorous theory building and modeling in this area, as well as simple lack of clarity and articulation in the literature.

PART 3. DOMINANCE AND COMPANION DOGS

In this section we will attempt to take the information we have explored so far and incorporate information specifically on domestic dogs to understand better how social dominance applies to dogs. I will start by presenting some general criticisms of the notion of social dominance. Then, I will describe social dominance as it applies to dogs in both dog - dog relationships and also in dog - human relationships. I will assess the value of social dominance as applied to dogs and explore alternatives.

Criticisms of Social Dominance

Many dog trainers and behavior consultants, researchers, theorists and academics in ethology challenge the usefulness and even validity of the various theories of social dominance. Since 1922 when social dominance was applied to vertebrates, many serious criticisms have been made regarding social dominance both in terms of validity as an ethological theory and also because of the usefulness of the idea. While many reject the theory outright, others find it useful in certain more narrow ethological contexts, and not in applied settings. Others continue to debate definitions of dominance and continue to research its features and mechanisms. Tilson (1981) outlines some general criticisms of social dominance. We will explore each of these criticisms and others below.

Contextual Complexity Reduces Predictive Value.

Many critics (e.g., Tilson, 1981; Chase, 1986) have pointed out that different measures of social dominance are poorly correlated (that is, they are not highly associated with one another statistically and so we might have two traits we consider related to dominance but then they do not usually occur together in individuals who we consider "dominant"). Some linear hierarchies, such as that found in (usually contrived) chicken societies, are very stable across contexts but this is far from universal. In many cases, an animal's status changes from context to context. A male wolf may be dominant in relation to others when it comes to food but then subordinate to a female when it comes to offspring rearing (Mech, 1999). Tilson sees it this way:

> The dominance concept loses its explanatory power when competitive orders change for each context. Little is gained by postulating a separate dominance order for each competitive situation, and a more parsimonious interpretation would be that individuals simply have different abilities to compete in each situation.

It is usually complicated to identify rank and hierarchies in groups from simply observing outcomes of dyadic conflicts. It becomes exponentially more complicated to identify ranking systems in multiple contexts. Surely there are other variables involved also. Say we devise a ranking system in a group of feral dogs living near a dump somewhere. Then (because it does not seem stable each time we measure it: unreliable), we decide to devise a separate ranking system for food, sleeping places, toys, mating opportunity etc. in order to improve the reliability of the measures the permutations, depending on the number of dogs in the group, becomes increasingly unmanageable. There may be sex differences and seasonal/hormonal differences also. We are still unlikely to see a strong positive correlation because of other situational variables. Say a dog that is usually subordinate in a given context is particularly well rested relative to an opponent in a particular contest. Perhaps we would see a role reversal here. Or say the dog is particularly hungry and more strongly motivated than his satiated opponent in a given encounter. The point is that motivational variables must also play into the model and the calculations become highly cumbersome if viable at all and if we seek a paired down simplistic model, it is likely to lack accuracy/reliability because of these complications. One goal of a good scientific model is to provide a simply way to see the process. Tilson (1981) continues:

> Dominance has been widely used as an interpretive concept because success in agonistic encounters is often correlated with increased access to food or mates. The fact that dominance rankings in different contexts are sometimes weakly correlated does not necessarily make the dominance concept useless, although it does point out deficiencies in overly simplistic notions of dominance.

What this suggests is that the fluid and contextual nature of outcome results in agonistic encounters makes it very difficult and cumbersome to determine a ranking system in anything but the simplest societies (e.g. with chickens). With the inclusion of context, one would expect more accurate predictive value although this sacrifices simplicity and determining exactly what constitutes appropriate contexts is challenging.

Artificial Social Dominance Hierarchies Generated by Captivity- and Crowding-Induced Stress

Social dominance hierarchies, in many cases, are a product of captivity and stress (Rowell, 1974). In other cases, "the hierarchy may be caused rather than revealed" (Rowell, 1974) by the artificial conditions arranged for in the studies. "At this point meaningless correlations may be found. Thus experimental findings which cannot be related to observations of behavior under natural conditions must be regarded with suspicion." (Rowell, 1974) It is repeatedly found that when a captive population is put together, artificial social dominance hierarchies are formed. Likely, these hierarchies are responses to abnormal social conditions. Much of the research done on wolves is done in captive, unrelated animals and the observations and conclusions are artificial and hence do not reflect the reality of real wolf packs—that is, they are invalid. The analogy is often made between the results of social principles of captive nonhuman animals and humans in concentration camps. You get abnormal relationships and generalizing that to more normal relationships is problematic at best.

Much of the mythology of social dominance in domestic dogs is assumed to be the same as in wolves because of their close evolutionary and genetic relationship. Even if 12,000 – 14,000 years of evolution did not change the sociability of the dog significantly, we cannot accept the observations of abnormal wolf behavior in non-wild conditions as evidence of how dogs behave.

Stress is prominent in captive animals. Stress is also a significant component of the experience of an animal losing an agonistic encounter. In the wild, stress is reduced by the animal's ability to avoid confrontation and also by the fact that they are not captive. In the wild, stress contributes to social dominance relationship formation and it is likely that in a highly stressful captive environment, social dominance relationships would form artificially. None of this is to suggest that social dominance relationships are only a product of captivity and stress but they influence it. In fact, social dominance relationships have been identified in natural animal populations, so dominance is not only a result of captivity.

Are dogs kept as pets in the home "captive"? Domestication has decreased flight distance and ease of socialization. In that regard, we cannot exactly consider dogs captive animals. Stress on the other hand may contribute to artificial social structure formation. There may be several variables that could contribute to stress-induced social behavior. Dogs living in multiple-dog households may experience a crowding stress or perhaps unusual conflicts of interests with other dogs. In the "wild," these dogs could avoid each other but in a house they cannot. It would seem that stress from various sources could contribute to social behavior suited to the stressful environment at hand. This could promote wildly variable social behavior that may not be easy to define and predict by theories of social dominance also.

Overemphasis on Aggression

Tilson (1981) offers this criticism of social dominance:

> Perhaps the most cogent criticism is that social dominance theory overemphasizes aggression as an organizing factor in social groups (see Loy, 1975; Bernstein, 1976). While many competitive situations are resolved in light of dominance relationships, affiliative ties based on shared interests are of crucial importance

for maintaining group cohesion and defining social relationships within groups. Social dominance theory should not be discarded, but dominance interactions should be viewed as just one of several ways that individuals pursue their own best interests within social groups.

This is a well-framed argument and one not frequently presented. Social dominance may prove useful under a limited set of circumstances (in perhaps a broad social-psychology context) but it should be seen in that light rather than a panacea, particular in applied settings.

Who Determined Contest Behavior?

Rowell (1974) has suggested that it might be more appropriate to refer to a "subordinance hierarchy" rather than a dominance hierarchy. She pointed out that (at least in captive baboons) it was the approach and retreat behaviors of subordinates that correlated best with rank while agonistic dominance behavior correlated significantly less so. Since then it is widely agreed that subordinates are more instrumental in guiding the course of interactions than the dominant animal. Assessment and learning are probably the mechanisms guiding this process. It seems just as appropriate to focus on preemptive deference as on who is exerting influence and control over others.

Wide Variety of Strategies and Social Structures

In many species, dominant animals are dominant because they are particularly aggressive and they use their skill and force to create fear in the other group members. But this is by no means universal. In many species the highest-ranking animal is tolerant of deference and so rarely ever needs to use aggressive tactics. There are a variety of strategies to maintain high rank. One animal may make extensive use of aggression and create fear while others may simply be more socially independent, encouraging other members who are less so to defer to them by way of their social reliance on them. In many cases, the highest-ranking animal may be fully prepared to defend consistent boundaries and so a system of learned pre-emptive deference organizes quickly and remains stable. In some cases, the highest-ranking animal may simply be the oldest or the largest and deference results from competitive assessment. The purpose of illustrating these various strategies is simply to point out that there may have evolved many strategies for group social structure organization. We may attempt to formulate a universal definition for social dominance but the strategies that a given society will actually use to achieve such organization, if they do at all, will be determined by natural selection and learning, and they are unlikely to all use the exact same process.

This sets up a very important problem faced by those who would like to apply social dominance to domestic dogs. Under what conditions do we wish to use social dominance with regards to dogs? What exactly is the actual environment for the dog? We have some data on feral and free-ranging dog populations but most companion dog guardians are more interested in the relationships between companion dogs, and also in the relationship between dogs and humans. They want a theory that explains what they see and that can be used, perhaps if they perceive relationship "problems" either between dogs or between dogs and humans. They are looking for a theory that will help guide their social relationships. This is an important topic that I will address more fully below. Are dogs that live together in a household a social group that we should look to for dominance relationships? Is it a society? If that is the social system to which we wish to generalize the results of our empirical observation then it might be more valid to look specifically at this social arrangement. What about groups of relatively strange dogs interacting in a dog park or a dog daycare or some similar environment? These two environments are likely to differ in some respects. These considerations must be observed if we are to look for social dominance systems in domestic dogs.

Comparing Wolves and Dogs

One of the biggest problems in the modern history of social dominance as it applies to domestic dogs is the direct transfer of conclusions made about wolf packs directly onto companion dogs. There are multiple problems with this approach. Some of these problems will be outlined below.

The first problem that comes to mind is the validity of applying conclusions drawn from wolf research onto another species. On the one hand, they share an evolutionary heritage. On the other hand there is a reason why dogs are not *Canis lupus* but rather *Canis familiaris*. They are not the same species and one of the primary reasons they evolved into a distinct group is because their sociability is different. Once they did start evolving into a separate group, artificial selection (a type of natural selection in which purposeful human selection is a primary selective pressure) created a further divergence of sociability. In the last 12,000 to 14,000 years or more, the domestic dog has gone its way, the wolf-like animal who was the ancestor of the present day animal we call a wolf has gone its. Can significant change in sociability take place in this amount of time? Belyaev's work with breeding foxes for biddability has demonstrated that significant changes in sociability can occur extremely quickly. Belyaev started with 465 foxes, breeding the quiet, exploratory ones rather than the fearful and aggressive ones (Coppinger & Coppinger, 2001). After eighteen generations (not a long time in evolutionary contexts) he had primarily a naturally tame animal, behaving much like the domestic dog (Coppinger & Coppinger, 2001).

> "They reacted to people actively and positively. They would search for their keepers, climb on them, take food from them, sit on the windowsill looking for someone to approach, roll over to get their tummies rubbed, and let people carry them around and give them their shots. They answered to their names." (Coppinger & Coppinger, 2001, p. 64)

Dogs are not wolves—that much is clear. But are they similar enough that it is valid to assume that what we learn about wild wolves in either captivity or the wild can be assumed to be the case for our domestic companion dog in our living room or in a dog park? I would argue that it may be of interest to ethologists to apply social dominance to dogs but it is not appropriate to assume that dogs will share a similar social structure to wolves. If we want to apply theories of social dominance to dogs and determine their particular manifestation of it then research is needed on dogs, not wolves. Wolf behavior will not answer our questions regarding the social behavior of dogs.

The second problem that comes to mind is the problem of wolf research itself. The prevailing view of wolf social behavior is based on myth, ignorance and on flawed research. Much of the research on the social behavior of wolves has been conducted on wolves in captivity and not on natural wolf packs in their natural environment (Mech, 1999). The results of these studies reflect highly contrived circumstances and may reflect abnormal or pathological behavior. Mech likens studying the social behavior of wolves in these environments to studying human social behavior by doing research in concentration camps. Mech describes a natural wolf pack as typically a family of related wolves (parents and the offspring). He describes them as a particularly nonviolent and orderly group that exists for a finite period of time before the offspring disperse, in which the parents are dominant (read parental) over the offspring, and the parents divide the contexts in which each is dominant over each other. Researchers observed strange (previously unknown to one another) and unrelated in crowded and capture-stressed wolves in these 'concentration camp' studies. The result was far more aggression and confinement-induced hierarchy formation. Unfortunately, a few dog trainers latched onto this early and problematic research. Lindsay (2001, p. 234) offers a telling quote from Konrad Most (1910/1955):

> In the pack of young dogs fierce fights take place to decide how they are to rank within the pack. And in a pack composed of men and dogs, canine competition for importance in the eyes of the trainer is keen. If this state of affairs is not countered by methods, which the canine mind can comprehend, it frequently ends in such animals attacking and seriously injuring not only their trainers, but also other people. As in a pack of dogs, the order of hierarchy in a man and dog combination can only be established by physical force—that is, by an actual struggle in which the man is instantaneously victorious. Such a result can only be brought about by convincing the dog of the absolute physical superiority of the man.

This statement is likely the result of these early flawed captive wolf studies and not likely from keen observation of actual dogs. In the wild and in living rooms, young dogs are not that aggressive. This kind of survival strategy might be observed in highly stressful, crowded groups of unrelated strange wolves but it is not typical of natural wolf behavior and certainly not of dog behavior. Also, how one interprets what they see depends on the theoretical orientation within which they work. If you were from a Freudian psychoanalytic school of thought you might see phallic symbols in everything you look at. Likewise a dominance-fixated dog trainer tends to see dominance in all dog behavior he or she sees. Science has shown that psychoanalytic theories are largely invalid and ineffective (Maxmen & Ward, 1995). So too is science demonstrating that social dominance may not be useful in many contexts it is applied to also.

Mech (1999) points out that "...no one has yet quantified the hierarchical relationships in a wild wolf pack." We do not know that much about the social behavior of wolves in terms of social dominance hierarchies. But Mech has offered us a clear picture of the social behavior of wolves in the summer months and it differs significantly from the myths created by old poorly designed studies of wolves in captivity. Mech (1999, p. 1202) concludes thusly about wolf society:

> The typical wolf pack, then, should be viewed as a family with the adult parents guiding the activities of the group and sharing group leadership in a division-of-labor system in which the female predominates primarily in such activities as pup care and defense and the male primarily during foraging and food-provisioning and travels associated with them...

Mech (1999) also points out that the "alpha" wolves are merely the breeding ones—the parents. He suggests it is no more appropriate to call these animals "alpha" than it is to use such terms as parent or breeder. These terms are not controversial and have clearly established meanings and so it seems clear that there is no use for the term "alpha" in that context. It provides low descriptive value.

It is important to note that Mech's (1999) study takes place only in summer months, which is when the wolves are at a relatively low point in their hormonal activity status, which may affect the ability to generalize results to other seasons (Beth Duman, March 2003, personal communication).

Within and Between Species Social Dominance

Dog – Dog Social Dominance Relationships

Urban, Rural and "Wild" Dog – Dog Relationships

The primary application of theories of social dominance would be to understanding the relationships between dogs. It, therefore, behooves us to explore the social behavior of dogs. Daniels and Bekoff (1989) report in their study of free-ranging dogs in urban and rural sites that "overall, there was a stronger tendency for dogs to avoid conspecifics than to group." These dogs tended to remain solitary, avoiding pack behavior, with a mean group size of 1.24 (variance 0.78) at one site, 1.10 (variance 0.61) at another site, 1.29 (variance 0.68) at a third site, and 1.32 (variance 0.65) at a fourth site. Rural group sizes were significantly larger than urban groups (Daniels & Bekoff, 1989). Daniels and Bekoff report that previous studies (e.g. Beck, 1973; Daniels, 1983) are consistent with their finding that urban and rural dogs tend to be solitary animals. "In addition, dogs probably were not as social as expected because little advantage was conferred on group-living animals. Scarce resources beyond those provided by human residents at both the urban and rural sites would be exploited more efficiently by individuals than by larger groups." (Daniels & Bekoff, 1989) It was found that feral ("wild") dogs were more likely to group than the urban or rural free-ranging dogs (Daniels & Bekoff, 1989). Daniels and Bekoff indicate that in these feral dogs group living may at times be advantageous but at other times be disadvantageous. The picture of the social behavior of dogs that emerges from this study indicates that free-ranging dogs in rural, urban and wild sites are not generally pack animals but rather solitary foragers. The groups that do form often involve adults and offspring prior to dispersal, are not large and adult members may be transient (joining and leaving with short duration of membership). It was not possible in this study to determine relatedness but given the presence of offspring it would seem likely that some relatedness was involved in-group formation. Basically it would seem that dog groups in the "wild" (urban, rural and wild) are loose associations and that group living is not usually advantageous and sometimes is for short duration.

Boitani, Francisci, Ciucci, and Andreoli, (1995) observed feral dog populations in central Italy. They define a pack as a social unit that hunts, rears young and protects a communal territory as a stable group. Boitani and colleagues describes the feral dogs they observed as meeting these criteria to only a limited extent, are not fully related, and that they do not follow the precise rules of pack living. They suggest the "the term 'group' seems more appropriate than pack." (Boitani et al., 1995, p. 233). Boitani and colleagues offer a great review of the literature:

> Two studies in Alabama reported group sizes of 2-5 and 2-6 individuals, respectively (Scott & Causey, 1973; Causey & Cude, 1980). Daniels & Bekoff (1989b) reported 2-4 animals per group in a feral population in Arizona, and Nesbitt (1975) found a mean group size of 5-6 animals, in his 5-year study of feral dogs in Illinois. Although Boitani & Racana (1984) observed feral dogs in Basilicata (southern Italy) mostly on pairs, the group size of 3-6 adults found in the present study (Fig. 15.10) tends to agree with those reported previously. Studies of urban free-ranging dogs report mainly solitary animals or pairs (Beck, 1975; Berman & Dunbar, 1983; Daniels, 1983a,b; Hirata, Okuzaki & Obara, 1986; Daniels & Bekoff, 1989b; Macdonald &Carr, Chapter 14), ...

What this indicates is that dogs, unlike wolves for example, are not strictly speaking, pack animals. But as discussed previously, animals group or pack to different degrees and in response to environmental needs. Some environments call for grouping as an individual survival strategy and other environments call for solitary or small group living. It would seem that urban and rural dogs tend to remain mainly solitary, and feral dogs tend to group a bit more. Boitani and colleagues (1995) suggest that existing social bonds with humans tend to decrease the dog's tendency to form other social contacts. The presence of predators such as wolves in feral versus urban and rural dog populations might tend to make grouping adaptive (Boitani et al., 1995). Increased vigilance and defense would contribute to this. They do report though that formed groups did tend to remain stable through their 3-year study.

Another interesting aspect of social behavior reported by Boitani and colleagues (1995) is that dogs "...stand alone, among canids in their total lack of paternal care..." (p. 235). The father does not help the female in raising young as wolves for example tend to, and domestication may have played a role in this social feature (Boitani, et al., 1995). This illustrates another situation in which wolves and dogs are not alike socially.

Yet another difference occurs in the context of mating. In wolf packs, one dominant female tends to mate and other females in the pack generally do not (with some exceptions). In these groups of dogs, there was no indication that any attempt to control the reproduction of any subordinate adult (Boitani, et al., 1995). "All females reproduced..." (Boitani, et al., 1995). The sociability of the wolf and the domestic dog seem significantly different in many aspects. One reason wolves pack is because it is adaptive for hunting large prey. In the Boitani and colleagues three-year study, they found no indication of predation on large prey. This may be one of many factors influencing the sociability and grouping or packing of the domestic dog versus the wolf.

Clearly, dogs are social animals. They play together and with us. They experience separation distress when left alone and seek us out for social stimulation, tolerating all sorts of shoddy treatment from us. The point for this section is to illustrate that in "nature," dogs are not pack animals living in organized societies. They are more solitary foragers at dumps and other food sources coming in contact to breed and occasionally for other purposes for brief duration. If you do not have to bring down a large prey animal or defend against dangerous predators then being in a group may not be necessary. The importance of this difference is that we cannot assume similarity in social behavior between wolves and dogs. Social dominance is a function of organized societies or group living. There is a lack of information on the exact nature of the social organization of these groups. It is tempting to speculate that the social organization is not as organized or stable as say a wolf pack—that they have the capability to tolerate others under specific circumstances but that generally speaking wild dogs are mostly solitary foragers. They are not hunting large ungulate prey, which is one reason to group worth mentioning also.

Companion Dog – Dog Relationships

Dogs living in households are usually solitary or with a single housemate. A smaller number of households have three or more dogs. Usually, the dogs are unrelated, and in many cases, members of different breeds and of different ages and sexes. We know that when we introduce two dogs they generally assess each other visually as well as by investigating each other in closer contact for indications of threat or affiliation. In many cases, play and other affiliative signals follow. It is possible that play may offer further assessment information as to the relative skill and strength of the opponent (Fagen, 1981). If one of the dogs offers appeasement or pre-emptive deference signals, the other dog will not usually respond with escalated aggressive signaling. If neither offers deference, escalation will sometimes occur. In other cases, both or one dog may simply disengage. If escalation occurs, a loud brief scuffle is common. These are usually ritualized and likely a part of the dog's assessment process. Usually, these assessment confrontations resolve with each gaining a better knowledge of each other. With each contact, each member appears to develop an expectation as to the likely outcomes of any potential competitive encounters. These change from context to context and with the relative individual motivational substrates of each animal so the process is complicated and difficult to predict, at least at first.

It is important to point out how territoriality can complicate social behavior in dogs. If one of the dogs is a resident and the other is a newcomer, the resident dog will often be motivated to defend their territory. Generally speaking, residents are more motivated and hence often win encounters even when the opponent is perhaps larger and otherwise would be expected to win. This is a common principle of behavioral ecology found in many species (Siiter, 1999). This can complicate prediction of the course of dog relationships by way of social dominance.

In triads, according to theories of social dominance, you can have transitive or intransitive relationships. A transitive system, if you remember is one in which A dominates B and B dominates C therefore A dominates C. Intransitive triads are ones in which A dominates B and B dominates C and C may dominate A. It becomes complicated because you may have to have one of these formulas for many different contexts as it may change significantly from context to context. There are other variables also, some of which we can attribute to motivation and other variables we cannot identify. At some point, the formula becomes so complex that it is an ever-changing and complex set of calculations to attempt a mathematical model of the relationships, thereby challenging the usefulness of the theory. The relationship evolves through time also. Some relationships seem easy to intuitively predict via social dominance and others impossible.

Furthermore, a similar assessment process governs the relationship between strange dogs on walks, in dog parks, in dog daycares and the like. Often social facilitation will complicate relationships. Groups of dogs will gang up on a newcomer for instance.

Dog – Human Dominance Relationships

As far as I know, there has been no solid research done on measuring social dominance between dogs and humans. Interspecies dominance is the basis for many popular books advising owners to dominate their dog (e.g., Baer and Duno, 1996). It is assumed by many that dominance relationships form between human and dog. What is needed is more research to illuminate these issues. At the moment, we know very little about how dominance relationships might form between dogs and humans. Certainly humans can highly effectively and efficiently teach dogs to behave in the way they want through manipulation of positive reinforcement so it remains unclear why a theory of social dominance would be required or even useful. In fact, it may simply distract us from recognizing the reinforcers that are maintaining behaviors in question and making simple changes in the reinforcement contingencies in order to change the behavior.

Social Dominance Fosters Adversarial Relationships Between Dogs and Their Guardians

As we have discussed, social dominance is all about exertion of control and influence. The very nature of the theory involves determining who is over or under whom, quantifying relationships in terms of who is the "alpha" or "boss." By using social dominance as a basis for how we interpret our dog's behavior or how we interact with our companion dogs, we conceptually frame the relationship in terms of the relationship between adversaries. It sets people in a zero-sum mindset, whereby someone must win at the expense of the other, that often leads to abuse. I am not saying that we should allow dogs to always do everything they want to do. We can manage the dog's environment and train the dog without need for social dominance models though; we can live in a win-win relationship rather than a win-lose one.

Dog guardians have been convinced that most of their dog's natural behaviors are signs that the dog is trying to stage a "regime change" and overthrow the leadership status in the family (as opposed to simply seeing dogs as maximizing reinforcers and minimizing punishers according to a behavioral model). There is widespread belief that dogs are status-seekers and if they are given half a chance, they will gain their alpha status and rule the household with an iron fist. People have twisted interpretations of many behaviors to fit with their theory that the dog is rank climbing. People have even managed to convince themselves that dogs are consciously seeking the alpha position for the sake of attaining the "position" as if what they want is the new title on top of the perks. This, of course, is highly anthropomorphic and unlikely. Seeking out evidence to support one's theory and ignoring evidence to the contrary is a cognitive bias and a major problem with many of those who insist on using social dominance in interpreting dog behavior.

The usual result of such adversarial relationships is a damaged safety history on the dog's part and a damaged bond between dog and guardian. How can you love an animal whom you are convinced is trying to usurp you—one that only cares about being "the boss"? It can also result in countercontrol, in which the dog learns from experience to work around the guardian in order to access reinforcers. The guardian purposely sets themselves as the obstacle between the dog and his or her reinforcers and so it is perfectly predictable that the dog will emit behaviors geared toward bypassing those obstacles. This is usually interpreted by the dominance-minded trainer or guardian as stubbornness and indeed manipulative status-seeking (dominance). It cannot be overstated how much damage theories of social dominance have done to the relationship between dogs and humans, and the dog is the one who suffers most of all because of such problems. There have been many attempts to educate the public on the dangers and value of social dominance theories (Donaldson, 1996; Bach, 1999; O'Heare, 2001, 2002, 2003, 2007, 2008) but the process is slow. This present work will be yet another attempt to explore the notion of social dominance, including its pitfalls.

Dominance and Aggression

A problem that theories of social dominance attempt to help us address is so called "dominance aggression." If it were not for the danger of aggressive behavior, social dominance would be far less of a concern (although mere disobedience is often blamed on social dominance also, rather than a simple lack of proper training as a behavioral approach would suggest). Many authors have attempted to get away from the dominance paradigm in order to minimize the misunderstanding associated with the term dominance. For example, Lindsay (2001) refers to "control related aggression." Donaldson (1996) prefers to discuss exactly what the dog is doing and what one would prefer the dog do, relying on training rather than rank reduction associated with social dominance theory. Bach (1999) also abandons dominance in explaining aggression. I (O'Heare, 2007, 2008) have made what I believe to be a compelling case for a behavioral approach rather than an ethological approach. A behavioral approach is interested not in categorical labels, and questionable and highly speculative "theories" of social behavior, but rather in measurable behaviors and the environmental variables that influence them (the contingencies that maintain behaviors). The behavioral approach is far more efficient and effective when it comes to explaining, predicting and changing behaviors. This will be discussed further below.

The phenomenon known variously as dominance aggression (Overall, 1997, p. 512) or control related aggression (Lindsay, 2001, p. 168) refers to a dog that inappropriately uses aggressive behavior in situations in which people passively or actively control the behavior of the dog. Certainly one can see that from a social dominance theoretical perspective, a socially dominant animal would be the more likely animal to control the behavior of others aggressively, while a subordinate animal would be far less likely. Of course, it depends on the scale you observe the phenomenon at. In a sense, subordinate dogs do control the behavior of the socially dominant dogs by the cut off and appeasement behaviors they use but this is not an aggressive control. On the other hand, the dominant dog might be expected to be intolerant of other animals taking things from them when they want them, "manhandling" them when they do not wish to be in that kind of contact or even just unloading frustration on them.

In the context of dog – dog interactions, what might a theory of social dominance offer us in terms of describing, explaining, predicting and dealing with such problem behavior? Social dominance (generously interpreted) would suggest to us that perhaps this dog has assessed the other dog or learned from previous encounters that he is the dominant member of the dyad and hence is not fearful of losing—he will be intolerant unless he receives deference signals. Is this hypothesis likely to pan out as an explanation? Perhaps it will, in some cases. In many cases, the dominant dog responds intolerantly to even the most minor imposition. The hypothesis does not hold up well.

Dominance Theory and Dogs

What does social dominance theory offer us in terms of predictive value? We would hypothesize that the primary aggression would occur between evenly matched dogs. As far as I know, this has not been studied empirically. Intuitively, we might not expect a very high level of predictive value in this case as many evenly matched dogs meet without escalation. Often, ritualized aggressive display is not even resorted to. In many cases, the dogs merely play. Defining 'evenly matched' operationally might help but in many cases, agonistic escalation does not occur in these encounters. Again, the hypothesis is shaky.

What other variables may play a role in the course of social contest relationships? It would seem some dogs are more motivated or seem to be in a hyper competitive mind set while others do not. Intuitively this would seem to be the functional variable involved. Without speculation as to the cognitive processes involved, it remains difficult to account for this variable. Perhaps we could identify determinants that we can correlate to our idea of a confident-competitive dog. If we could find reliable indicator behaviors that are directly observable, we could work this into the theory and a higher predictive value could be achieved. This remains to be seen. At present, this is explained adequately with the behavioral principle of motivating operations, those conditions that make a reinforcer more or less valuable and hence the operants that access them as more or less likely.

Why use the term social dominance? Can the interactions and relationships between dogs be accounted for by another established and more parsimonious theory? The trend seems to be to get away from dominance-talk and to rather refer to such component features as display/assessment, control, defense, resource possession etc. In a behavioral approach, contingencies between motivation, behaviors and consequences are employed.

In the context of dog – human relationships, what do social dominance theories offer us? There is no research on this topic that I know of. It is conceivable that dogs perceive human family members as a social group and in that context apply their organizing social behaviors. It is conceivable that dogs assess us in some way and when motivated to be intolerant of being controlled they use aggressive behaviors. Why must we use the term dominance to describe this? Why not simply say that a particular dog is intolerant of being controlled or that he has a relatively low threshold for aggression? Or better, why not simply identify the specific behaviors in question for a particular dog as well as the consequences that are maintaining them and then change those consequences? The dominance alternative is to postulate that the dog believes he or she is dominant in the relationship. This may or may not be the case. It might simply mean that the dog has either assessed himself to be superior or has learned via previous encounters that the human will defer. Again, why is this dominance-talk necessary or helpful? Why not explain the behavior in terms of the very well established and non-speculative principles of learning and behavior? A behavioral approach is our primary tool of changing such behavior and so it would seem to make intuitive sense that we use the same theory to explain and predict such behavior. We can expect animals to maximize reinforcers and minimize punishers. The science of behavior and it's principles of learning account for all of these behaviors clearly and concisely, offering extremely high descriptive, explanatory and predictive value, offering a clear set of principles for addressing the problem. Positively reinforcing behavior one wants to see more of, and failing to reinforce unwanted behavior suffers little or no fallout, which is common when invoking dominance theory.

Alternative Approaches to Explaining, Predicting and Changing the Social Behavior of Dogs

Although I have mentioned at alternatives to theories of social dominance in describing, explaining and predicting behavior in general and social behavior specifically in previous sections, I would like here to elaborate on those points more completely.

Social dominance is an ethological theory, perhaps useful in explaining why we observe so little fatal and damaging aggressive behavior within groups of predator species that live in societies. In that social-psychology context, it seems to be useful. The trouble has come from using the theory of social dominance as the basis for describing and explaining social relationships between dogs, and dogs and people because of its emphasis on an adversarial mindset. This basic cognitive mindset has resulting in abuse as people attempt to apply the notion of social dominance to finding solutions to problem behaviors or merely how to interact with their companion dog. Simply, they are told to dominate the dog. In the strongest interpretation of this approach, people are told to physically dominate the dog, forcibly rolling them onto their backs and staring them down until the "say uncle," or grabbing them by the muzzle or scruff of the neck and shaking them to reassert one's dominion over them. In a weaker interpretation, they are told to psychologically dominate the dog. In this case, they often prefer the term leadership to dominance. In this variant, the guardian is told to frustrate the dog's attempts to control just about anything and they are required to instate a kind of dog boot camp wherein the dog is required to perform specific behaviors and defer before receiving anything desirable to them. They are "put in their place" either physically or psychologically. In both variants, and whether you call it leadership or dominance, it is still derivative of social dominance, which implies adversarial win-lose encounters and relationships. Even if you try to frame this in terms of leadership, the result is similar because one cannot help but infer this underlying win-lose principle from the theory; it's an assumption of most common formulations of the theory. What is needed is not a softer variant, but a more productive theory with less problematic assumptions from which to derive a way to describe, explain and change behavior.

Given the significant lack of empirical evidence to support the effectiveness of applying social dominance theories to changing behavior and the questionable, speculative nature of its ability to explain or predict much of what it is commonly used for, what is needed is a model of behavior that is not speculative but rather scientific, not lacking in empirical evidence but supported by a strong history of scientific evidence. A better choice of model should be effective and efficient in explaining, predicting and changing behavior. The approach that best meets these criteria is a behavioral approach, or behavior analytic approach if you prefer. The behavioral approach focuses on observable and measurable behavior and its relationship to the environment. A behavioral approach makes use of the principles of operant and respondent conditioning, which have been shown scientifically to be highly effective at explaining, predicting and changing behavior through thousands upon thousands of properly conducted experimental studies (as opposed to extremely limited naturalistic observational studies that cannot identify causal relationships among variables). Respondent behaviors (reflexive behaviors) and respondent conditioning can explain emotional responses that motivate operants (consequence driven behaviors), and are the basis for general behavior traits (behavioral tendencies strongly influenced by genetics). Reinforcement (increase in frequency of a behavior due to consequences) maintains operants and punishment (decrease in frequency of behavior due to consequences) can suppress operants, as we know.

How can this be applied to the social behavior of dogs? Social behavior, just like any other behavior, operates in accordance with the principles of learning and as such it can be explained and predicted. In simple lay-terms, dogs do what works to get them what they want and they avoid or escape things they find unpleasant. If they wish to affiliate with another dog, they will use communication signals that convey that message and hope that their partner reciprocates. If they have a pleasant experience with the other dog, this will become associated with that individual and the probability of their affiliative behavior will increase in frequency in the future. If they have an unpleasant experience, that will become associated with that individual and they can be expected to avoid or escape that kind of encounter in the future. In that case, many use appeasement signals to convey that they intend no harm and wish to avoid escalated aggressive interactions. Each encounter contributes to the type of emotional response the dog will have to that other individual and hence contribute to the motivation for the operants they choose. In conflicts of interests, for example when you ask them to get off the bed, or another dog wants their toy, or you pet one dog while ignoring another who would like some petting too, operants are used to access these contingencies. The dog can be expected to perform behaviors that work to access reinforcers and avoid or escape punishers. All social behaviors can be explained quite effectively and far more parsimoniously and less speculatively by referencing the simple principles of respondent and operant conditioning than social dominance. It is also verifiable in that these predictions can be empirically tested and logically determined to be accurate or inaccurate reflections of reality. Because of the vagueness of social dominance in various applications, it is rarely testable and often evidence to the contrary is ignored while just about any outcome (even an outcome and its opposite) are taken as evidence to support it. For example, guardians are commonly told that when a dog goes out of the door before them, that this is a "sign" of dominance. The guardian is instructed to assert their dominance over the dog. If the dog is bullied into waiting (explained easily by aversive conditioning) then social dominance is supposedly supported. If not, the guardian is told they simply did not dominate the dog enough. If they never manage to dominate the dog enough, the dog is considered intractably dominant and in some cases, is killed.

This example brings me to changing behavior. In the above example, it is much less speculative and much more parsimonious to hypothesize that the dog simply values getting outside as soon as possible and there was no reason not to just go. Being outside, or getting to the "bathroom" or a toy or whatever is the actual reinforcer is, is accessed by the walking out of the door behavior. There is no competing reinforcement and so the behavior is performed. The beauty of explaining the behavior in a behavioral manner is that the explanation helps suggest a means of changing that behavior if you want to. If, for some reason, you would rather the dog wait for you to get out of the door first (perhaps for safety reasons if the dog might knock you over) then you know you can manipulate the contingencies involved. You can make it so that charging out ahead of you does not work while sitting patiently does work. With some repetition and consistency, the dog's rushing out behavior is decreased in favor of the sitting behavior, which is increased in frequency. Once we identify the antecedent stimuli that set the occasion for the behavior, motivate it and indicate that a particular schedule of reinforcement is in effect, and also the consequences that result from the behavior (and ABCs of behavior) we have a strong and verifiable understanding of the behavior and also the basis for a behavior change procedure. Instead of speculating about social dominance in situations such as these, we could be asking ourselves what is the dog getting out of this behavior or what is he escaping or avoiding? Our hypothesized answer can be tested empirically with a functional analysis (a real world experiment to identify the actual contingencies maintaining the behavior) and when we know for sure, we can simply change the contingency to change the behavior.

If, and to the extent that, social dominance "works" in any given instance, the likely reason is that the contingencies were accidentally changed in the process. For instance, the dog might find your assertion of dominance to be so unpleasant that he or she suppresses the behavior that has led to it in order to escape or avoid that experience again. This heavy-handed technique will often result in problematic secondary effects. Aversive conditioning can easily lead to learned helplessness, aggression and countercontrol (as the dog learns how to work around the unpleasant experiences in order to access the still present reinforcers). Countercontrol is often interpreted as stubbornness and further indication that the dog is dominant and the vicious cycle perpetuates itself. In the less heavy-handed practice of instating a Nothing In Life Is Free (NILIF) program, guardians are instructed to ensure that the dogs gets nothing for free. This is often a part of "leadership" training, but saying that the dog comes to realize that they are the follower and you are the leader is basically the same as saying you are exerting your dominance over the subordinate dog. The guardian is instructed to ensure that all good things in life for the dog are allowed but only after the dog has obeyed some command first. This practice can sometimes work to change specific behaviors but inefficiently because it is convoluted with dominance connotations. It works to the extent that it is incidentally taking advantage of the principles of learning. Certainly taking frequent opportunities to train the dog, making real life reinforcers contingent on performance of specific behaviors will change behaviors. If you ask a dog to sit before getting his dinner, you have an opportunity to train a good solid sit and that goes for the various other behaviors used. We do not need to invoke notions of dominance or leadership for this. The whole notion of NILIF connotes an adversarial relationship to many. Even when explained without reference to dominance or even leadership, people commonly infer a boot camp approach in this practice. If the dog performs behaviors that the guardian finds unacceptable, it is inefficient to take the round about way of working through some leadership program such as NILIF. It is much more efficient and effective to get right to the issue, identify the contingencies maintaining that behavior and change them. Make it worth the dog's while to perform some replacement behavior rather than the problem behavior. Do you want to take more frequent opportunity to train the dog? No problem. Guardians can be instructed on how to identify reinforcers and make them contingent on performance of certain behaviors in order to train those behaviors to a higher degree of reliability.

If we could try to get ourselves into a behavioral mindset of recognizing the contingencies that are maintaining the behaviors we observe on an ongoing basis, rather than into a social dominance mindset of who is over or under whom, we could more effectively explain and change behaviors. To explain the course of social relationships and the behaviors used in encounters between individuals we can look to how pleasant or unpleasant the experiences are and the reinforcers that the dog seeks to access. If the experiences are unpleasant then we can expect escape or avoidance behaviors (be they flight, appeasement or preemptive attack even, depending on what works best) and if we want to change this behavior we can change the association between the other individual and the experience they have with them. If we make experiences pleasant rather than unpleasant then escape and avoidance behaviors will not be motivated. At the same time, we can make acceptable behaviors work well and the problem behavior either work less well (inefficient and irrelevant). This is achieved through simply changing the contingencies.

This is by no means a complete introduction to the principles of learning (and it was written in a conversational style rather than a technical manner) but it will serve to support my argument that a behavioral approach is more parsimonious, empirically supported and more efficient and effective than any social dominance theory at explaining and changing behavior. If those interested in social dominance spent as much time learning about the principles of learning as they did speculating on the dominance relationships involved, they would likely be far closer to improving the bond between them and their dog or between their dog and other dogs and in achieving fewer problem behaviors in favor of more acceptable behaviors

Conclusion

What conclusions can we draw from our exploration of social dominance? Social dominance has been devised to help explain why we observe very little damaging aggression among members of societies, particularly in predatory species that are capable of killing each other. In that regard, social dominance has been somewhat successful but this success is ethological or social-psychological. At some point, dog trainers discovered the theory and attempted to apply it to explaining the interactions between dogs and between dogs and people. They also sought to use it to suggest ways to interact with dogs and resolve problem behaviors. The theory was not intended for this but it was a very attractive model to many people and it became a fad. Little or no research was done to substantiate the usefulness of the notion and cognitive bias promoted ignoring of anecdotal evidence to its contrary while accepting almost all evidence as supporting. In ethology, it would seem that theories of social dominance could have some explanatory value. In our living rooms and dog parks, it seems to be of far less value. What it has demonstrated is that it can do great harm to companion dogs through misguided application or simply by distracting us to the obvious behavioral explanations. We can understand the social behavior of dogs without reference to social dominance by making use of the principles of learning and behavior. Rather than setting up a zero-sum game whereby there must be a winner and loser, a cooperative win-win scenario can be set up instead.

My proposal is to acknowledge the purpose for social dominance as a theory for explaining the lack of aggression within societies but not apply it inappropriately. When it comes to explaining and changing behavior, the principles of learning and behavior are vastly more successful and will promote a more enjoyable bond between dogs and people. In the end, in applied settings, I suggest dropping social dominance all together.

BIBLIOGRAPHY

Bold citations indicate excellent sources of information for further study.

Abrantes, R. (1997). Dog Language An Encyclopedia Of Canine Behaviour., Special revised and updated English version ed.Naperville, Illinois: Wakan Tanka Publishers.

Adams, D. B. (1979). Brain mechanisms for offense, defense, and submission. The Behavioral and Brain Sciences 2,201-241.

Allee, W. C. (1942). Social dominance and subordination among vertebrates. Biological Symposia 8,139-162.

Aloff, Brenda. (2002). Aggression in Dogs Practical management, Prevention & Behaviour Modification. Fundcraft, Inc. Collierville TN.

Appleby, M. C. 1979. The probability of linearity in hierarchies. The Behavioral and Brain Sciences 2,201-241.

Baenniger, R. (1981). Dominance: On distinguishing the baby from the bathwater. Behavioral and Brain Sciences, 4, 431–432.

Baer, N. and Duno, S. (1996). Leader of the Pack. Harper. N.Y. New York.

Barash, D. P. (2003). The survival game: How game theory explains the biology of cooperation and competition. New York: Times Books.

Barrette, C. (1993). The 'inheritance of dominance', or of an aptitude to dominate. Animal Behaviour. 46,591-593.

Barrette, C., and D. Vandal. (1986). Social rank, dominance, antler size, and access to food in snow-bound wild woodland caribou. Behaviour 97,118-146:

Beach F. A., Buehler M. G., and Dunbar I .F. (1982). Competitive behavior in male, female, and pseudohermaphroditic female dogs. Journal of Comparative Physiological Psychology 96,855-874.

Beaugrand, J. P. (1977). Relative importance of initial individual differences, agonistic experience, and assessment accuracy during hierarchy formation: A simulation study. Behavioural Processes 41,177-192.

Beaugrand, J. P. (1997). Relative importance of initial individual differences, agonistic experience, and assessment accuracy during hierarchy formation: a simulation study. Behavioral Processes 41,177-192.

Beaugrand, J. P., and C. Goulet. (2000). Distinguishing kinds of prior dominance and subordination experiences in male Green swordtail fish (Xiphophorus helleri). Behavioural Processes 50,131-142.

Begin, J., P. J. Beaugrand, and R. Zayan. (1996). Selecting dominants and subordinates at conflict outcome can confound the effects of prior dominance or subordination experience. Behavioral Processes 36,219-226.

Bekoff, M. (1972). The development of social interaction, play, and metacommunication in mammals: An ethological perspective. Quarterly Review Biology 47,412-434.

Bekoff, M. (1977). Social communication in canids: Evidence for the evolution of a stereotyped mammalian display. Science 197,1097-1099.

Bekoff, M., and C. Allen. (1998). Intentional communication and social play: how and why animals negotiate and agree to play. in Animal Play Evolutionary, Comparative, and Ecological Perspectives by Bekoff and Byers (Ed.) Cambridge Press

Bekoff, M., and C. Allen. (2002). The evolution of social play: interdisciplinary analyses of cognitive processes. in The Cognitive Animal. Bekoff, M., Allen, C. and Burghardt, G.M. (Ed) 429-435.

Bernstein, I. S., and Gordon T.P. (1980). The social component of dominance relationships in rhesus monkeys. Animal Behaviour 28,1033-1039.

Bernstein, I. S. (1981). Dominance: the baby and the bath water. The Behavioral and Brain Sciences 4,419-457.

Boitani, L., Francisci, F., Ciucci, P., and Andreoli, G. (1995). Population biology and ecology of feral dogs in central Italy. In The Domestic Dog its evolution, behaviour and interactions with people, Serpell, J. (Ed). Chapter 15, pp.218-244.

Brown, J. L. (1963). Aggressiveness dominance and social organization in the steller jay. Condor 65,460-484.

Capitanio, J. P. (1991). Levels of integration and the 'inheritance of dominance'. Animal Behaviour 42,495-496.

Carr, G. M., and D. W. Macdonald. (1986). The sociality of solitary foragers: a model based on resource dispersion. Animal Behaviour 34,1540-1549.

Chance, P. (1988). Learning and Behavior 2nd. Ed. Wadsworth Publishing Company. Belmont CA.

Chase, I. D. (1974). Models of hierarchy formation in animal societies. Behavioral Science 19,374-382.

Chase, I. D. (1982). Behavioral sequences during dominance hierarchy formation in chickens. Science 216,439-440.

Chase, I. D. (1985). Explanations of hierarchy structure. Animal Behaviour 34,1265-1266.

Chase, I. D., C. Bartolomeo, and L. A. Dugatkin. (1994). Aggressive interactions and inter-contest interval: how long do winners keep winning? Animal Behaviour 48,393-400.

Christian, J. (1970). social subordination, population density and mammalian evolution. Science 168,84-90.

Clarke, R. S., W. Heron, M. L. Fetherstonehaugh, D. G. Forgays, and D. O. Hebb. (1951). Individual differences in dogs: preliminary report on the effects of early experience. Canadian Journal of Psychology 5(4),150-156.

Clothier, S. Hard to train? Retrieved March 28, 2003 http://www.flyingdogpress.com/difficult.html

Clothier, S. Of hostages & relationships. Retrieved March 28, 2003 http://www.flyingdogpress.com/

Clothier, S. Why not take candy from a baby (if he lets you?). Retrieved March 28, 2003 http://www.flyingdogpress.com/candy.html

Collias, N. E. (1943). Statistical analysis of factors which make for success in initial encounters between hens. American Naturalist 77,519-538.

Copi, M. I. (1986). Introduction to logic (7th ed.). New York: MacMillan Publishing Company.

Coppinger, R. (1983). The domestication of evolution. Environmental Conservation, 10(4), 283-292.

Coppinger, R., and L. Coppinger. 2001. Dogs A Startling New Understanding of Canine Origin, Behavior & Evolution. New York, NY: Scribner.

Daniels, T. J., and M. Bekoff. (1989). Population and social biology of free-ranging dogs, Canis familiaris. Journal of Mammalogy 70(4),754-762.

de Waal, F. B. M. (1986). The interaction of dominance and social bonding in primates. Quarterly Review of Biology 61(4),459-479.

de Waal, F. B. M. (2000). The first kiss foundations of conflict resolution research in animals. In F. Aureli & F. B. M. de Waal (Eds.), Natural conflict resolution (pp. 15–33). Berkeley and Los Angeles: California University Press.

Deag, M. J. (1977). Aggression and submission in monkey society. Animal Behaviour 25,465-474.

Denenberg, V. H., and J. R. C. Morton. (1962). Effects of environmental complexity and social groupings upon modification of emotional behavior. Journal of Comparative and Physiological Psychology 55(2),242-246.

Dewsbury, D. A. (1990). Fathers and sons: genetic factors and social dominance in deer mice, Peromyscus maniculatus. Animal Behaviour 39,284-289.

Dewsbury, D. A. (1991). Genes influence behaviour. Animal Behaviour 42,499-500.

Donaldson, J. (1996). The Culture Clash. James and Kenneth Publishers. Oakville, Ontario.

Drews, C. (1993). The concept and definition of dominance in animal behaviour. Behaviour 125(3-4),283-313.

Duman, B. (2003). Some thoughts on letting go of the dominance paradigm in training dogs. Retrieved March 28, 2003 http://www.dogpsych.com/thoughtsondominance.pdf

Eaton, Barry. (2002). Dominance: Fact or Fiction? Berks, Great Britton.

Encarta.com (n.d.). Retrieved October 19, 2004, from http://encarta.msn.com/encnet/features/dictionary/dictionaryhome.aspx

Enquist, M. (1985). Communication during aggressive interactions with particular reference to variation in choice of behavior. Animal Behaviour 33,1152-1161.

Fagan, R. (1981). Animal Play Behavior. Oxford University Press.

Fentress, J. C. (1967). Observations on the behavioral development of a hand-reared male timber wolf. American Zoologist 7,339-351.

Fogelin, R. J. (1987). Understanding arguments: An introduction to informal logic (3rd ed.). Toronto, Canada: Harcourt Brace Jovanovich, Inc.

Fox, M. W. (1970). A comparative study of the development of facial expressions in canids; wolf, coyotes and foxes. Behaviour 36,49-73.

Fox, M. W., and D. Stelzner. (1966). Behavioural effects of differential early experience in the dog. Animal Behaviour 14,273-281.

France, C. B. (2001). Appeasing pheromones in mammals. World Small Animal Veterinary Association World Congress - Vancouver 2001

Frank, H., and Frank, M. G. (1982). On the effects of domestication on canine social development and behavior. Applied Animal Ethology, 8, 507-525.

Gage, F. H. (1978). A multivariate approach to the analysis of social dominance. Behavioral Biology 23,38-51.

Gese, E. M. ,., and L. D. Mech. 1991. Dispersal of wolves (Canis lupus) in northeastern Minnesota 1969-1989. Canadian Journal of Zoology 69,2946-2955.

Grant, E. C., and J. H. Mackintosh. (1958). A comparison of the social postures of some common laboratory rodents. Behaviour 21,246-259.

Guilford, T., and M. S. Dawkins. (1991). Receiver psychology and the evolution of animal signals. Animal Behavior. 42,1-14.

Hand, J. L. (1986). Resolution of social conflict: Dominance, egalitarianism, spheres of dominance, and game theory. The Quarterly Review of Biology, 61(2), 201–220.

Hare, B., Brown, M., Williamson, C., and Tomasello, M. (2002). The domestication of social cognition of dogs. Science, 298, 1634-1636

Hill, H. L., and M. Bekoff. (1977). The variability of some motor components of social play and agonistic behavior in infant eastern coyotes, Canis latrans var. Animal Behavior. 25,907-909.

Hinde, R. A., & Datta, S. (1981). Dominance: An intervening variable. Behavioral and Brain Sciences, 4, 442.

Hsu, Y., and L. L. Wolf. (2001). The winner and loser effect: what fighting behaviours are influenced? Animal Behavior. 61,777-786.

Jackson, W. M., and R. L. Winnegrad. (1988). Linearity in dominance hierarchy: a second look at the individual attribute model. Animal Behaviour 36,1237-1240.

James, W. T. (1955). Behaviors involved in expression of dominance among puppies. Psychological Reports 1,299-301.

Kaplan, J. R. (1981). A reexamination of dominance rank and hierarchy in primates. The Behavioral and Brain Sciences 4,442-443.

Kleiman, D. G. (1967). Some aspects of the social behavior in the Canidae. Animal Zoology. 7,365-372.

Lehrman, D. S. (1953). A critique of Konrad Lorenz's theory of instinctive behavior. The Quarterly Review of Biology 28(4),337-363.

Lewontin, R. C. (1979). Sociobiology as an adaptationist program. Behavioral Sciences 24,5-14.

Lindsay, S. R. (2001). Handbook of Applied Dog Behavior and Training volume two. Iowa University State Press. Ames, Iowa.

Lindstrom, E. (1986). Territory inheritance and the evolution of group-living in carnivores. Animal Behaviour 34,1825-1835.

Little, F. J., Groarke, L. A., & Tindale, C. W. (1998). Good reasoning matters: A constructive approach to critical thinking. Toronto, Canada: McClellend & Stewart Inc.

London, K. B., McConnell, P. B. (2001). Feeling Outnumbered? How to manage and Enjoy Your Muti-Dog Household. Dog's Best Friend, Ltd. Black Earth, WI.

Macdonald, D. W. (1983). The ecology of carnivore social behaviour. Nature 301,379-384.

Maxman, J., and Ward, N. (1995). Essential Psychopathology and Its Treatment 2nd Ed. W.W. Norton & Company. New York, NY.

Mazur, A. (1973). A cross-species comparison of status in small established groups. American Sociological Review 38(5),513-530.

Mazur, A., and A. Booth. (1998). Testosterone and Dominance in Men. Behavioural and Brain Sciences at 21,353-363.

McFarland, D. (1999). Animal Behaviour 3rd edition. Prentice Hall. Essex, England.

Mech, D. L. (1995). Summer Movements and behavior of an arctic wolf, Canis lupus, pack without pups. The Canadian Field-Naturalist 109,473-475.

Mech, D. L. (1999). Alpha status, dominance, and division of labor in wolf packs. Canadian Journal of Zoology 77,1196-1203.

Mech, D. L., and M. E. Nelson. (1990). Non-family wolf, Canis lupus, packs. The Canadian Field-Naturalist 104,482-483.

Mech, L. D., P. C. Wolf, and J. M. Packard. (1999). Regurgitative food transfer among wild wolves. Canadian Journal of Zoology 77,1192-1195.

Messier, F. (1985). Solitary living and extraterritorial movements of wolves in relation to social status and prey abundance. Canadian Journal of Zoology 63,239-245.

Mineka, S. (1979). The role of fear in theories of avoidance learning, flooding and extinction. Psychological Bulletin 86(5),985-1010.

Moore, A. J. (1984). The evolution of reciprocal sharing. Ethology and Sociobiology 5,5-14.

Moore, A. J. (1991). Genetics, inheritance and social behaviour. Animal Behaviour 42,497-498.

Moore, A. J. (1990). The inheritance of social dominance, mating behaviour and attractiveness to mates in male Nauphoeta cinerea. Animal Behaviour 39,388-397.

Morse, D. H. (1974). Niche breadth as a function of social dominance. The American Naturalist 108(964),818-830.

Moyer, K. E. (1968). Kinds of aggression and their physiological basis. Communications in Behavioral Biology, Part A 2,65-87.

Noll, D. E. (1999). The neuropsychology of human conflict. Retrieved March 28, 2003 http://www.manageconflict.com/Neuropsy.htm

O'Heare, J. (2001). The Canine Aggression Workbook 1st edition. DogPsych Publishing. Ottawa.

O'Heare, J. (2002). Review and critique of pack theory models and an introduction to alternative models of domestic dog social behavior. Journal of the Academy of Canine Behavioral Theory, 1(1),16-28

O'Heare, J. (2003). The Canine Aggression Workbook 2nd edition. DogPsych Publishing. Ottawa.

O'Heare, J. (2003). Canine Neuropsychology 2nd edition. DogPsych Publishing. Ottawa.

Onelook.com (n.d.). Retrieved December 28, 2005, from http://www.onelook.com/?w=familiar&ls=a

Onelook.com1 (n.d.). Retrieved December 28, 2005, from http://www.onelook.com/?w=power&ls=a

Osborne, M. J. (2004). An introduction to game theory. New York: Oxford University Press.

Overall, K. L. (1997). Clinical Behavioral Medicine for Small Animals. Mosby. St. Louis, Missouri.

Packard, J. M., L. M. Mech, and R. R. Ream. (1992). Weaning in an artic wolf pack: behavioural mechanisms. Canadian Journal of Zoology 70,1269-1275.

Parker, G. A. (1974). Assessment strategy and the evolution of fighting behaviour. Journal of Theoretical Biology, 47, 223–243.

Pollock, G. B., and S. W. Rissing. (1988). Social competition under mandatory group life in The Ecology of Social Behavior by Slobodchikoff, C.N. (Ed). California: Academic Press.

Preuschoft, S., & van Schaik, C. P. (2000). Dominance and communication conflict management in various social settings. In F. Aureli, and F. B. M. de Waal (Eds.), Natural conflict resolution (pp. 77–105). Berkeley and Los Angeles: California University Press.

Price, E. O. (1984). Behavioral aspects of animal domestication. The Quarterly Review of Biology, 59(1), 1-32.

Pulliainen, E. (1967). A contribution to the study of the social behavior of the wolf. American Zoologist. 7,313-317.

Pusey, A. E., and C. Packer. (1997). The ecology of relationships in Behavioural Ecology an evolutionary approach 4th. ed by Krebs, John R. and Davies, Nicholas B. (Eds). Oxford: Blackwell Science.

Rabb, G. B. (1967). Social relationships in a group of captive wolves. American Zoologist 7,305-311.

Reisner, I. (1998). Canine aggression: neurobiology, behavior and management. Retrieved March 28, 2003 http://www.vetshow.com/friskies/cani.htm

Rowell, T. E. (1966). Hierarchy in the organization of a captive baboon group. Animal Behaviour 14,430-443.

Rowell, T. E. (1974). The concept of dominance. Behavioral Biology 11,131-154.

Rugaas, Turid. (1997). On Talking Terms with Dogs: Calming Signals. Legacy By Mail. Carlsborg, WA

Schenkel, R. (1967). Submission: its features and function in the wolf and dog. American Zoologist 7,319-329.

Scott, J. P. (1948). Dominance and the frustration-aggression hypothesis. Physiological Zoology 21,31-39.

Scott, J. P. (1962). Critical periods in behavioral development. Science 138,949-957.

Scott, J. P. (1967). The evolution of social behavior in dogs and wolves. American Zoologist 7,373-381.

Scott, J. P. and Fuller, J. L. (1965). Genetics and the Social Behavior of the Dog. The University of Chicago Press. Chicago.

Serpell, J. (Ed). (1995). The Domestic Dog its evolution, behaviour and interactions with people. Cambridge University Press. Cambridge, UK.

Siiter, R. (1999). Introduction to Animal Behavior. Brooks/Cole Publishing. Toronto.

Stebbins, R. C. and Cohen, N. W. (1995). A Natural History of Amphibians. Princeton University Press. Princeton, NJ.

Snow, C. J. (1967). Some observations on the behavioral and morphological development of coyote pups. American Zoologist 7,353-355.

Szamado, S. (2000). Cheating as a mixed strategy in a simple model of aggressive communication. Animal Behaviour 59,221-230.

Thompson, K. V. (1998). Self assessment in juvenile play. Animal Play Evolutionary, Comparative, and ecological Perspectives. Cambridge Press

Thorpe, K. E., A. C. Taylor, and F. A. Huntingford. (1995). How costly is fighting? Physiological effects of sustained exercise and fighting in swimming crabs, Necora puber (L.) (Brachyura, Portunidae). Animal Behaviour 50,1657-1666.

Tilson, R. (1981). Animal Social Behavior Chapter 13. Duxbury Press.

Tinbergen, N. (1974). Ethology and stress diseases. Science 185,20-27.

Uyeno, E. T., and M. White. (1967). Social Isolation and dominance behavior. Journal of Comparative and Physiological Psychology 63(1),157-159.

Wethey, and Woodin, Ecology and Evolution: Biology 301 Fall 2002. Retrieved April 8, 2003 from http://www.biol.sc.edu/~wethey/301/NaturalSelection.html

Van Ballenberghe, V. (1983). extraterritorial movements and dispersal of wolves in southcentral Alaska. Journal of Mammalogy 64(1),168-171.

Vessey, S. H. (1981). Dominance as control. Behavioral and Brain Sciences, 4, 449.

Von Schantz, T. (1984). Carnivore social behaviour--does it need patches? Nature 307,389-390.
Wikipedia.org1 (n.d.). Retrieved October 19, 2004, from http://en.wikipedia.org/wiki/Circular_definition
Wikipedia.org2 (n.d.). Retrieved October 19, 2004, from http://en.wikipedia.org/wiki/Tautology
Wikepedia.org3 (n.d.). Retrieved October 19, 2004, from http://en.wikipedia.org/wiki/Fallacies_of_definition
Wilson, E. O. (1975). Sociobiology The New Synthesis. The Belknap Press. Cambridge Massachusetts.